CREATIVE UNITY

CREATIVE UNITY

RABINDRANATH TAGORE

GYAN

Published by

GYAN

Gyan Publishing House
5, Ansari Road
Daryaganj, New Delhi-110002
Phone: 011-47034999, 9811692060
E mail: books@gyanbooks.com

Distribution Network
gyanbooks.com
India, USA, Canada, UK, Australia, France

ISBN: 978-81-212-9372-3 (PB)
First Published, 1922

2nd Impression 2023

Printed at: Gyan Press, Delhi.

CREATIVE UNITY

AUTHOR: RABINDRANATH TAGORE

CREATIVE UNITY

CREATIVE UNITY

BY

RABINDRANATH TAGORE

MACMILLAN AND CO., LIMITED
ST. MARTIN'S STREET, LONDON
1922

TO

DR. EDWIN H. LEWIS

INTRODUCTION

It costs me nothing to feel that I am; it is no burden to me. And yet if the mental, physical, chemical, and other innumerable facts concerning all branches of knowledge which have united in myself could be broken up, they would prove endless. It is some untold mystery of unity in me, that has the simplicity of the infinite and reduces the immense mass of multitude to a single point.

This One in me knows the universe of the many. But, in whatever it knows, it knows the One in different aspects. It knows this room only because this room is One to it, in spite of the seeming contradiction of the endless facts contained in the single fact of the room. Its knowledge of a tree is the knowledge of a unity, which appears in the aspect of a tree.

This One in me is creative. Its creations are a pastime, through which it gives expression to an ideal of unity in its endless show of variety. Such are its pictures, poems, music, in which it finds joy only because they reveal the perfect forms of an inherent unity.

This One in me not only seeks unity in knowledge for its understanding and creates images of unity for its delight; it also seeks union in love for its fulfilment. It seeks itself in others. This is a fact, which would be absurd had there been no great medium of truth to give it reality. In love we find a joy which is ultimate because it is the ultimate truth. Therefore it is said in the Upanishads that the *advaitam* is *anantam*,—"the One is Infinite"; that the *advaitam* is *anandam*,—"the One is Love."

To give perfect expression to the One, the Infinite, through the harmony of the many; to the One, the Love, through the sacrifice of self, is the object alike of our individual life and our society.

CONTENTS

THE POET'S RELIGION

THE POET'S RELIGION

I

Civility is beauty of behaviour. It requires for its perfection patience, self-control, and an environment of leisure. For genuine courtesy is a creation, like pictures, like music. It is a harmonious blending of voice, gesture and movement, words and action, in which generosity of conduct is expressed. It reveals the man himself and has no ulterior purpose.

Our needs are always in a hurry. They rush and hustle, they are rude and unceremonious; they have no surplus of leisure, no patience for anything else but fulfilment of purpose. We frequently see in our country at the present day men utilising empty kerosene cans for carrying water. These cans are emblems of discourtesy; they are curt and abrupt, they have not the least shame for their unmannerliness, they do not care to be ever so slightly more than useful.

The instruments of our necessity assert that we must have food, shelter, clothes, comforts and convenience. And yet men spend an immense amount of their time and resources in contradicting this assertion, to prove that they are not a mere living catalogue of endless wants; that there is in them an ideal of perfection, a sense of unity, which is a harmony between parts and a harmony with surroundings.

The quality of the infinite is not the magnitude of extension, it is in the *Advaitam*, the mystery of Unity. Facts occupy endless time and space; but the truth comprehending them all has no dimension; it is One. Wherever our heart touches the One, in the small or the big, it finds the touch of the infinite.

I was speaking to some one of the joy we have in our personality. I said it was because we were made conscious by it of a spirit of unity within ourselves. He answered that he had no such feeling of joy about himself, but I was sure he exaggerated. In all probability he had been suffering from some break of harmony between his surroundings and the spirit of unity within him, proving all the more strongly its truth. The meaning of health comes home to us with painful force when disease disturbs it; since health expresses the unity of the vital functions and is accordingly joyful. Life's tragedies occur, not to demonstrate their own reality, but to reveal that eternal principle of joy in life, to which they gave a rude shaking. It is the object of this Oneness in us to realise its infinity by perfect union of love with others. All obstacles to this union create misery, giving rise to the baser passions that are expressions of finitude, of that separateness which is negative and therefore *máyá*.

The joy of unity within ourselves, seeking expression, becomes creative; whereas our desire for the fulfilment of our needs is constructive. The water vessel, taken as a vessel only, raises the question, "Why does it exist at all?" Through its fitness of construction, it offers the apology for its existence. But where it is a work of beauty it has no question to answer; it has nothing to do, but to be. It reveals in its form a unity to which all that seems various in it is so related that, in a mysterious manner, it strikes sympathetic chords to the music of unity in our own being.

What is the truth of this world? It is not in the masses of substance, not in the number of things, but in their relatedness, which neither can be counted, nor measured, nor abstracted. It is not in the materials which are many, but in the expression which is one. All our knowledge of things is knowing them in their relation to the Universe, in that relation which is truth. A drop of water is not a particular assortment of elements; it is the miracle of a harmonious mutuality, in which the two reveal the One. No amount of analysis can reveal to us this mystery of unity. Matter is an abstraction; we shall never be able to realise what it is, for our world of reality does not acknowledge it. Even the giant forces of the world, centripetal and centrifugal, are kept out of our recognition. They are the day-labourers not admitted into the audience-hall of creation. But light and sound come to us in their gay dresses as troubadours singing serenades before the windows of the senses. What is constantly before us, claiming our attention, is not the kitchen, but the feast; not the anatomy of the world, but its countenance. There is the dancing ring of seasons; the elusive play of lights and shadows, of wind and water; the many-coloured wings of erratic life flitting between birth and death. The importance of these does not lie in their existence as mere facts, but in their language of harmony, the mother-tongue of our own soul, through which they are communicated to us.

We grow out of touch with this great truth, we forget to accept its invitation and its hospitality, when in quest of external success our works become unspiritual and unexpressive. This is what Wordsworth complained of when he said:

> The world is too much with us; late and soon,
> Getting and spending, we lay waste our powers.
> Little we see in Nature that is ours.

But it is not because the world has grown too familiar to us; on the contrary, it is because we do not see it in its aspect of unity, because we are driven to distraction by our pursuit of the fragmentary.

Materials as materials are savage; they are solitary; they are ready to hurt one another. They are like our individual impulses seeking the unlimited freedom of wilfulness. Left to themselves they are destructive. But directly an ideal of unity raises its banner in their centre, it brings these rebellious forces under its sway and creation is revealed—the creation which is peace, which is the unity of perfect relationship. Our greed for eating is in itself ugly and selfish, it has no sense of decorum; but when brought under the ideal of social fellowship, it is regulated and made ornamental; it is changed into a daily festivity of life. In human nature sexual passion is fiercely individual and destructive, but dominated by the ideal of love, it has been made to flower into a perfection of beauty, becoming in its best expression symbolical of the spiritual truth in man which is his kinship of love with the Infinite. Thus we find it is the One which expresses itself in creation; and the Many, by giving up opposition, make the revelation of unity perfect.

II

I remember, when I was a child, that a row of cocoanut trees by our garden wall, with their branches beckoning the rising sun on the horizon, gave me a companionship as living as I was myself. I know it was my imagination which transmuted the world around me into my own world—the imagination which seeks unity, which deals with it. But we have to consider that this companionship was true; that the universe in which I was born had in it an element profoundly akin to my own imaginative mind, one which wakens in all children's natures the Creator, whose pleasure is in interweaving the web of creation with His own patterns of many-coloured strands. It is something akin to us, and therefore harmonious to our imagination. When we find some strings vibrating in unison with others, we know that this sympathy carries in it an eternal reality. The fact that the world stirs our imagination in sympathy tells us that this creative imagination is a common truth both in us and in the heart of existence. Wordsworth says:

> I'd rather be
> A pagan suckled in a creed outworn;
> So might I, standing on this pleasant lea,
> Have glimpses that would make me less forlorn;
> Have sight of Proteus rising from the sea,
> Or hear old Triton blow his wreathèd horn.

In this passage the poet says we are less forlorn in a world which we meet with our imagination. That can only be possible if through our imagination is revealed, behind all appearances, the reality which gives the touch of companionship, that is to say, something which has an affinity to us. An immense amount of our activity is engaged in making images, not for serving any useful purpose or formulating rational propositions, but for giving varied responses to the varied touches of this reality. In this image-making the child creates his own world in answer to the world in which he finds himself. The child in us finds glimpses of his eternal playmate from behind the veil of things, as Proteus rising from the sea, or Triton blowing his wreathèd horn. And the playmate is the Reality, that makes it possible for the child to find delight in activities which do not inform or bring assistance but merely express. There is an image-making joy in the infinite, which inspires in us our joy in imagining. The rhythm of cosmic motion produces in our mind the emotion which is creative.

A poet has said about his destiny as a dreamer, about the worthlessness of his dreams and yet their permanence:

> I hang 'mid men my heedless head,
> And my fruit is dreams, as theirs is bread:
> The goodly men and the sun-hazed sleeper,
> Time shall reap; but after the reaper
> The world shall glean to me, me the sleeper.

The dream persists; it is more real than even bread which has substance and use. The painted canvas is durable and substantial; it has for its production and transport to market a whole array of machines and factories. But the picture which no factory can produce is a dream, a *máyá*, and yet it, not the canvas, has the meaning of ultimate reality.

A poet describes Autumn:

> I saw old Autumn in the misty morn
> Stand shadowless like Silence, listening
> To silence, for no lonely bird would sing
> Into his hollow ear from woods forlorn.

Of April another poet sings:

> April, April,
> Laugh thy girlish laughter;
> Then the moment after
> Weep thy girlish tears!
> April, that mine ears
> Like a lover greetest,
> If I tell thee, sweetest,
> All my hopes and fears.
>
> April, April,
> Laugh thy golden laughter.
> But the moment after
> Weep thy golden tears!

This Autumn, this April,—are they nothing but phantasy?

Let us suppose that the Man from the Moon comes to the earth and listens to some music in a gramophone. He seeks for the origin of the delight produced in his mind. The facts before him are a cabinet made of wood and a revolving disc producing sound; but the one thing which is neither seen nor can be explained is the truth of the music, which his personality must immediately acknowledge as a personal message. It is neither in the wood, nor in the disc, nor in the sound of the notes. If the Man from the Moon be a poet, as can reasonably be supposed, he will write about a fairy imprisoned in that box, who sits spinning fabrics of songs expressing her cry for a far-away magic casement opening on the foam of some perilous sea, in a fairyland forlorn. It will not be literally, but essentially true. The facts of the gramophone make us aware of the laws of sound, but the music gives us personal companionship. The bare facts about April are alternate sunshine and showers; but the subtle blending of shadows and lights, of murmurs and movements, in April, gives us not mere shocks of sensation, but unity of joy as does music. Therefore when a poet sees the vision of a girl in April, even a downright materialist is in sympathy with him. But we know that the same individual would be menacingly angry if the law of heredity or a geometrical problem were described as a girl or a rose—or even as a cat or a camel. For these intellectual abstractions have no magical touch for our lute-strings of imagination. They are no dreams, as are the harmony of bird-songs, rain-washed leaves glistening in the sun, and pale clouds floating in the blue.

The ultimate truth of our personality is that we are no mere biologists or geometricians; "we are the dreamers of dreams, we are the music-makers." This dreaming or music-making is not a function of the lotus-eaters, it is the creative impulse which makes songs not only with words and tunes, lines and colours, but with stones and metals, with ideas and men:

> With wonderful deathless ditties
> We build up the world's great cities,
> And out of a fabulous story
> We fashion an empire's glory.

I have been told by a scholar friend of mine that by constant practice in logic he has weakened his natural instinct of faith. The reason is, faith is the spectator in us which finds the meaning of the drama from the unity of the performance; but logic lures us into the greenroom where there is stagecraft but no drama at all; and then this logic nods its head and wearily talks about disillusionment. But the greenroom, dealing with its fragments, looks foolish when questioned, or wears the sneering smile of Mephistopheles; for it does not have the secret of unity, which is somewhere else. It is for faith to answer, "Unity comes to us from the One, and the One in ourselves opens the door and receives it with joy." The function of poetry and the arts is to remind us that the greenroom is the greyest of illusions, and the reality is the drama presented before us, all its paint and tinsel, masks and pageantry, made one in art. The ropes and wheels perish, the stage is changed; but the dream which is drama remains true, for there remains the eternal Dreamer.

III

Poetry and the arts cherish in them the profound faith of man in the unity of his being with all existence, the final truth of which is the truth of personality. It is a religion directly apprehended, and not a system of metaphysics to be analysed and argued. We know in our personal experience what our creations are and we instinctively know through it what creation around us means.

When Keats said in his "Ode to a Grecian Urn":

> Thou, silent form, dost tease us out of thought,
> As doth eternity, . . .

he felt the ineffable which is in all forms of perfection, the mystery of the One, which takes us beyond all thought into the immediate touch of the Infinite. This is the mystery which is for a poet to realise and to reveal. It comes out in Keats' poems with struggling gleams through consciousness of suffering and despair:

> Spite of despondence, of the inhuman dearth
> Of noble natures, of the gloomy days,
> Of all the unhealthy and o'er-darken'd ways
> Made for our searching: yes, in spite of all,
> Some shape of beauty moves away the pall
> From our dark spirits.

In this there is a suggestion that truth reveals itself in beauty. For if beauty were mere accident, a rent in the eternal fabric of things, then it would hurt, would be defeated by the antagonism of facts. Beauty is no phantasy, it has the everlasting meaning of reality. The facts that cause despondence and gloom are mere mist, and when through the mist beauty breaks out in momentary gleams, we realise that Peace is true and not conflict, Love is true and not hatred; and Truth is the One, not the disjointed multitude. We realise that Creation is the perpetual harmony between the infinite ideal of perfection and the eternal continuity of its realisation; that so long as there is no absolute separation between the positive ideal and the material obstacle to its attainment, we need not be afraid of suffering and loss. This is the poet's religion.

Those who are habituated to the rigid framework of sectarian creeds will find such a religion as this too indefinite and elastic. No doubt it is so, but only because its ambition is not to shackle the Infinite and tame it for domestic use; but rather to help our consciousness to emancipate itself from materialism. It is as indefinite as the morning, and yet as luminous; it calls our thoughts, feelings, and actions into freedom, and feeds them with light. In the poet's religion we find no doctrine or injunction, but rather the attitude of our entire being towards a truth which is ever to be revealed in its own endless creation.

In dogmatic religion all questions are definitely answered, all doubts are finally laid to rest. But the poet's religion is fluid, like the atmosphere round the earth where lights and shadows play hide-and-seek, and the wind like a shepherd boy plays upon its reeds among flocks of clouds. It never undertakes to lead anybody anywhere to any solid conclusion; yet it reveals endless spheres of light, because it has no walls round itself. It acknowledges the facts of evil; it openly admits "the weariness, the fever and the fret" in the world "where men sit and hear each other groan"; yet it remembers that in spite of all there is the song of the nightingale, and "haply the Queen Moon is on her throne, and there is:

> White hawthorn, and the pastoral eglantine,
> Fast-fading violets covered up in leaves;
> And mid-day's eldest child,
> The coming musk-rose, full of dewy wine,
> The murmurous haunt of flies on summer eves.

But all this has not the definiteness of an answer; it has only the music that teases us out of thought as it fills our being.

Let me read a translation from an Eastern poet to show how this idea comes out in a poem in Bengali:

> In the morning I awoke at the flutter of thy boat-sails,
> Lady of my Voyage, and I left the shore to follow the beckoning waves.
> I asked thee, "Does the dream-harvest ripen in the island beyond the blue?"
> The silence of thy smile fell on my question like the silence of sunlight on waves.
> The day passed on through storm and through calm,
> The perplexed winds changed their course, time after time, and the sea moaned.
> I asked thee, "Does thy sleep-tower stand somewhere beyond the dying embers of the day's funeral pyre?"

No answer came from thee, only thine eyes smiled like
the edge of a sunset cloud.

It is night. Thy figure grows dim in the dark.
Thy wind-blown hair flits on my cheek and thrills my
sadness with its scent.

My hands grope to touch the hem of thy robe, and
I ask thee—"Is there thy garden of death beyond the
stars, Lady of my Voyage, where thy silence
blossoms into songs?"

Thy smile shines in the heart of the hush like the
star-mist of midnight.

IV

In Shelley we clearly see the growth of his religion through periods of vagueness and doubt, struggle and searching. But he did at length come to a positive utterance of his faith, though he died young. Its final expression is in his "Hymn to Intellectual Beauty." By the title of the poem the poet evidently means a beauty that is not merely a passive quality of particular things, but a spirit that manifests itself through the apparent antagonism of the unintellectual life. This hymn rang out of his heart when he came to the end of his pilgrimage and stood face to face with the Divinity, glimpses of which had already filled his soul with restlessness. All his experiences of beauty had ever teased him with the question as to what was its truth. Somewhere he sings of a nosegay which he makes of violets, daisies, tender bluebells and—

> That tall flower that wets,
> Like a child, half in tenderness and mirth,
> Its mother's face with heaven-collected tears.

He ends by saying:

> And then, elate and gay,
> I hastened to the spot whence I had come,
> That I might there present it!—Oh! to whom?

This question, even though not answered, carries a significance. A creation of beauty suggests a fulfilment, which is the fulfilment of love. We have heard some poets scoff at it in bitterness and despair; but it is like a sick child beating its own mother—it is a sickness of faith, which hurts truth, but proves it by its very pain and anger. And the faith itself is this, that beauty is the self-offering of the One to the other One.

In the first part of his "Hymn to Intellectual Beauty" Shelley dwells on the inconstancy and evanescence of the manifestation of beauty, which imparts to it an appearance of frailty and unreality:

> Like hues and harmonies of evening,
> Like clouds in starlight widely spread,
> Like memory of music fled.

This, he says, rouses in our mind the question:

> Why aught should fail and fade that once is shown,
> Why fear and dream and death and birth
> Cast on the daylight of this earth
> Such gloom,—why man has such a scope
> For love and hate, despondency and hope?

The poet's own answer to this question is:

> Man were immortal, and omnipotent,
> Didst thou, unknown and awful as thou art,
> Keep with thy glorious train firm state within his heart.

This very elusiveness of beauty suggests the vision of immortality and of omnipotence, and stimulates the effort in man to realise it in some idea of permanence. The highest reality has actively to be achieved. The gain of truth is not in the end; it reveals itself through the endless length of achievement. But what is there to guide us in our voyage of realisation? Men have ever been struggling for direction:

> Therefore the names of Demon, Ghost, and Heaven
> Remain the records of their vain endeavour,
> Frail spells,—whose uttered charm might not avail to sever,
> From all we hear and all we see,
> Doubt, chance and mutability.

The prevalent rites and practices of piety, according to this poet, are like magic spells—they only prove men's desperate endeavour and not their success. He knows that the end we seek has its own direct call to us, its own light to guide us to itself. And truth's call is the call of beauty. Of this he says:

> Thy light alone,—like mist o'er mountain driven,
> Or music by the night wind sent,
> Thro' strings of some still instrument,
> Or moonlight on a midnight stream
> Gives grace and truth to life's unquiet dream.

About this revelation of truth which calls us on, and yet which is everywhere, a village singer of Bengal sings:

> My master's flute sounds in everything,
> drawing me out of my house to everywhere.
> While I listen to it I know that every step I take
> is in my master's house.
> For he is the sea, he is the river that leads to the sea,
> and he is the landing place.

Religion, in Shelley, grew with his life; it was not given to him in fixed and ready-made doctrines; he rebelled against them. He had the creative mind which could only approach Truth through its joy in creative effort. For true creation is realisation of truth through the translation of it into our own symbols.

V

For man, the best opportunity for such a realisation has been in men's Society. It is a collective creation of his, through which his social being tries to find itself in its truth and beauty. Had that Society merely manifested its usefulness, it would be inarticulate like a dark star. But, unless it degenerates, it ever suggests in its concerted movements a living truth as its soul, which has personality. In this large life of social communion man feels the mystery of Unity, as he does in music. From the sense of that Unity, men came to the sense of their God. And therefore every religion began with its tribal God.

The one question before all others that has to be answered by our civilisations is not what they have and in what quantity, but what they express and how. In a society, the production and circulation of materials, the amassing and spending of money, may go on, as in the interminable prolonging of a straight line, if its people forget to follow some spiritual design of life which curbs them and transforms them into an organic whole. For growth is not that enlargement which is merely adding to the dimensions of incompleteness. Growth is the movement of a whole towards a yet fuller wholeness. Living things start with this wholeness from the beginning of their career. A child has its own perfection as a child; it would be ugly if it appeared as an unfinished man. Life is a continual process of synthesis, and not of additions. Our activities of production and enjoyment of wealth attain that spirit of wholeness when they are blended with a creative ideal. Otherwise they have the insane aspect of the eternally unfinished; they become like locomotive engines which have railway lines but no stations; which rush on towards a collision of uncontrolled forces or to a sudden breakdown of the overstrained machinery.

Through creation man expresses his truth; through that expression he gains back his truth in its fulness. Human society is for the best expression of man, and that expression, according to its perfection, leads him to the full realisation of the divine in humanity. When that expression is obscure, then his faith in the Infinite that is within him becomes weak; then his aspiration cannot go beyond the idea of success. His faith in the Infinite is creative; his desire for success is constructive; one is his home, and the other is his office. With the overwhelming growth of necessity, civilisation becomes a gigantic office to which the home is a mere appendix. The predominance of the pursuit of success gives to society the character of what we call *Shudra* in India. In fighting a battle, the *Kshatriya*, the noble knight, followed his honour for his ideal, which was greater than victory itself; but the mercenary *Shudra* has success for his object. The name Shudra symbolises a man who has no margin round him beyond his bare utility. The word denotes a classification which includes all naked machines that have lost their completeness of humanity, be their work manual or intellectual. They are like walking stomachs or brains, and we feel, in pity, urged to call on God and cry, "Cover them up for mercy's sake with some veil of beauty and life!"

When Shelley in his view of the world realised the Spirit of Beauty, which is the vision of the Infinite, he thus uttered his faith:

> Never joy illumed my brow
> Unlinked with hope that thou wouldst free
> This world from its dark slavery;
> That thou,—O awful Loveliness,—
> Wouldst give whate'er these words cannot express.

This was his faith in the Infinite. It led his aspiration towards the region of freedom and perfection which was beyond the immediate and above the successful. This faith in God, this faith in the reality of the ideal of perfection, has built up all that is great in the human world. To keep indefinitely walking on, along a zigzag course of change, is negative and barren. A mere procession of notes does not make music; it is only when we have in the heart of the march of sounds some musical idea that it creates song. Our faith in the infinite reality of Perfection is that musical idea, and there is that one great creative force in our civilisation. When it wakens not, then our faith in money, in material power, takes its place; it fights and destroys, and in a brilliant fireworks of star-mimicry suddenly exhausts itself and dies in ashes and smoke.

VI

Men of great faith have always called us to wake up to great expectations, and the prudent have always laughed at them and said that these did not belong to reality. But the poet in man knows that reality is a creation, and human reality has to be called forth from its obscure depth by man's faith which is creative. There was a day when the human reality was the brutal reality. That was the only capital we had with which to begin our career. But age after age there has come to us the call of faith, which said against all the evidence of fact: "You are more than you appear to be, more than your circumstances seem to warrant. You are to attain the impossible, you are immortal." The unbelievers had laughed and tried to kill the faith. But faith grew stronger with the strength of martyrdom and at her bidding higher realities have been created over the strata of the lower. Has not a new age come to-day, borne by thunder-clouds, ushered in by a universal agony of suffering? Are we not waiting to-day for a great call of faith, which will say to us: "Come out of your present limitations. You are to attain the impossible, you are immortal"? The nations who are not prepared to accept it, who have all their trust in their present machines of system, and have no thought or space to spare to welcome the sudden guest who comes as the messenger of emancipation, are bound to court defeat whatever may be their present wealth and power.

This great world, where it is a creation, an expression of the infinite—where its morning sings of joy to the newly awakened life, and its evening stars sing to the traveller, weary and worn, of the triumph of life in a new birth across death,—has its call for us. The call has ever roused the creator in man, and urged him to reveal the truth, to reveal the Infinite in himself. It is ever claiming from us, in our own creations, co-operation with God, reminding us of our divine nature, which finds itself in freedom of spirit. Our society exists to remind us, through its various voices, that the ultimate truth in man is not in his intellect or his possessions; it is in his illumination of mind, in his extension of sympathy across all barriers of caste and colour; in his recognition of the world, not merely as a storehouse of power, but as a habitation of man's spirit, with its eternal music of beauty and its inner light of the divine presence.

THE CREATIVE IDEAL

THE CREATIVE IDEAL

In an old Sanskrit book there is a verse which describes the essential elements of a picture. The first in order is *Vrúpa-bhédáh*—"separateness of forms." Forms are many, forms are different, each of them having its limits. But if this were absolute, if all forms remained obstinately separate, then there would be a fearful loneliness of multitude. But the varied forms, in their very separateness, must carry something which indicates the paradox of their ultimate unity, otherwise there would be no creation.

So in the same verse, after the enumeration of separateness comes that of *Pramānāni*—proportions. Proportions indicate relationship, the principle of mutual accommodation. A leg dismembered from the body has the fullest licence to make a caricature of itself. But, as a member of the body, it has its responsibility to the living unity which rules the body; it must behave properly, it must keep its proportion. If, by some monstrous chance of physiological profiteering, it could outgrow by yards its fellow-stalker, then we know what a picture it would offer to the spectator and what embarrassment to the body itself. Any attempt to overcome the law of proportion altogether and to assert absolute separateness is rebellion; it means either running the gauntlet of the rest, or remaining segregated.

The same Sanskrit word *Pramānāni*, which in a book of æsthetics means proportions, in a book of logic means the proofs by which the truth of a proposition is ascertained. All proofs of truth are credentials of relationship. Individual facts have to produce such passports to show that they are not expatriated, that they are not a break in the unity of the whole. The logical relationship present in an intellectual proposition, and the æsthetic relationship indicated in the proportions of a work of art, both agree in one thing. They affirm that truth consists, not in facts, but in harmony of facts. Of this fundamental note of reality it is that the poet has said, "Beauty is truth, truth beauty."

Proportions, which prove relativity, form the outward language of creative ideals. A crowd of men is desultory, but in a march of soldiers every man keeps his proportion of time and space and relative movement, which makes him one with the whole vast army. But this is not all. The creation of an army has, for its inner principle, one single idea of the General. According to the nature of that ruling idea, a production is either a work of art or a mere construction. All the materials and regulations of a joint-stock company have the unity of an inner motive. But the expression of this unity itself is not the end; it ever indicates an ulterior purpose. On the other hand, the revelation of a work of art is a fulfilment in itself.

The consciousness of personality, which is the consciousness of unity in ourselves, becomes prominently distinct when coloured by joy or sorrow, or some other emotion. It is like the sky, which is visible because it is blue, and which takes different aspect with the change of colours. In the creation of art, therefore, the energy of an emotional ideal is necessary; as its unity is not like that of a crystal, passive and inert, but actively expressive. Take, for example, the following verse:

Oh, fly not Pleasure, pleasant-hearted Pleasure,
Fold me thy wings, I prithee, yet and stay.
    For my heart no measure
    Knows, nor other treasure
To buy a garland for my love to-day.

And thou too, Sorrow, tender-hearted Sorrow,
Thou grey-eyed mourner, fly not yet away.
    For I fain would borrow
    Thy sad weeds to-morrow,
To make a mourning for love's yesterday.

The words in this quotation, merely showing the metre, would have no appeal to us ; with all its perfection and its proportion, rhyme and cadence, it would only be a construction. But when it is the outer body of an inner idea it assumes a personality. The idea flows through the rhythm, permeates the words and throbs in their rise and fall. On the other hand, the mere idea of the above-quoted poem, stated in unrhythmic prose, would represent only a fact, inertly static, which would not bear repetition. But the emotional idea, incarnated in a rhythmic form, acquires the dynamic quality needed for those things which take part in the world's eternal pageantry.

Take the following doggerel :

Thirty days hath September,
April, June, and November.

The metre is there, and it simulates the movement of life. But it finds no synchronous response in the metre of our heart-beats; it has not in its centre the living idea which creates for itself an indivisible unity. It is like a bag which is convenient, and not like a body which is inevitable.

This truth, implicit in our own works of art, gives us the clue to the mystery of creation. We find that the endless rhythms of the world are not merely constructive; they strike our own heart-strings and produce music.

Therefore it is we feel that this world is a creation; that in its centre there is a living idea which reveals itself in an eternal symphony, played on innumerable instruments, all keeping perfect time. We know that this great world-verse, that runs from sky to sky, is not made for the mere enumeration of facts—it is not "Thirty days hath September"—it has its direct revelation in our delight. That delight gives us the key to the truth of existence; it is personality acting upon personalities through incessant manifestations. The solicitor does not sing to his client, but the bridegroom sings to his bride. And when our soul is stirred by the song, we know it claims no fees from us; but it brings the tribute of love and a call from the bridegroom.

It may be said that in pictorial and other arts there are some designs that are purely decorative and apparently have no living and inner ideal to express. But this cannot be true. These decorations carry the emotional motive of the artist, which says: "I find joy in my creation; it is good." All the language of joy is beauty. It is necessary to note, however, that joy is not pleasure, and beauty not mere prettiness. Joy is the outcome of detachment from self and lives in freedom of spirit. Beauty is that profound expression of reality which satisfies our hearts without any other allurements but its own ultimate value. When in some pure moments of ecstasy we realise this in the world around us, we see the world, not as merely existing, but as decorated in its forms, sounds, colours and lines; we feel in our hearts that there is One who through all things proclaims: "I have joy in my creation."

That is why the Sanskrit verse has given us for the essential elements of a picture, not only the manifoldness of forms and the unity of their proportions, but also *bhávah*, the emotional idea.

It is needless to say that upon a mere expression of emotion—even the best expression of it—no criterion of art can rest. The following poem is described by the poet as "An earnest Suit to his unkind Mistress":

> And wilt thou leave me thus?
> Say nay, say nay, for shame!
> To save thee from the blame
> Of all my grief and grame.
> And wilt thou leave me thus?
> Say nay! say nay!

I am sure the poet would not be offended if I expressed my doubts about the earnestness of his appeal, or the truth of his avowed necessity. He is responsible for the lyric and not for the sentiment, which is mere material. The fire assumes different colours according to the fuel used; but we do not discuss the fuel, only the flames. A lyric is indefinably more than the sentiment expressed in it, as a rose is more than its substance. Let us take a poem in which the earnestness of sentiment is truer and deeper than the one I have quoted above:

> The sun,
> Closing his benediction,
> Sinks, and the darkening air
> Thrills with the sense of the triumphing night,—
> Night with her train of stars
> And her great gift of sleep.
> So be my passing!
>
> My task accomplished and the long day done,
> My wages taken, and in my heart
> Some late lark singing,

> Let me be gathered to the quiet West,
> The sundown splendid and serene,
> Death.

The sentiment expressed in this poem is a subject for a psychologist. But for a poem the subject is completely merged in its poetry, like carbon in a living plant which the lover of plants ignores, leaving it for a charcoal-burner to seek.

This is why, when some storm of feeling sweeps across the country, art is under a disadvantage. In such an atmosphere the boisterous passion breaks through the cordon of harmony and thrusts itself forward as the subject, which with its bulk and pressure dethrones the unity of creation. For a similar reason most of the hymns used in churches suffer from lack of poetry. For in them the deliberate subject, assuming the first importance, benumbs or kills the poem. Most patriotic poems have the same deficiency. They are like hill streams born of sudden showers, which are more proud of their rocky beds than of their water currents; in them the athletic and arrogant subject takes it for granted that the poem is there to give it occasion to display its powers. The subject is the material wealth for the sake of which poetry should never be tempted to barter her soul, even though the temptation should come in the name and shape of public good or some usefulness. Between the artist and his art must be that perfect detachment which is the pure medium of love. He must never make use of this love except for its own perfect expression.

In everyday life our personality moves in a narrow circle of immediate self-interest. And therefore our feelings and events, within that short range, become prominent subjects for ourselves. In their vehement self-assertion they ignore their unity with the All. They rise up like obstructions and obscure their own background. But art gives our personality the disinterested freedom of the eternal, there to find it in its true perspective. To see our own home in flames is not to see fire in its verity. But the fire in the stars is the fire in the heart of the Infinite; there, it is the script of creation.

Matthew Arnold, in his poem addressed to a nightingale, sings:

> Hark! ah, the nightingale—
> The tawny-throated!
> Hark, from that moonlit cedar what a burst!
> What triumph! hark!—what pain!

But pain, when met within the boundaries of

limited reality, repels and hurts; it is discordant with the narrow scope of life. But the pain of some great martyrdom has the detachment of eternity. It appears in all its majesty, harmonious in the context of everlasting life; like the thunder-flash in the stormy sky, not on the laboratory wire. Pain on that scale has its harmony in great love; for by hurting love it reveals the infinity of love in all its truth and beauty. On the other hand, the pain involved in business insolvency is discordant; it kills and consumes till nothing remains but ashes.

The poet sings again:

> How thick the bursts come crowding through the leaves!
> Eternal Passion!
> Eternal Pain!

And the truth of pain in eternity has been sung by those Vedic poets who had said, "From joy has come forth all creation." They say:

> Sa tapas tapatvá sarvam asrajata Yadidam kincha.
>
> (God from the heat of his pain created all that there is.)

The sacrifice, which is in the heart of creation, is both joy and pain at the same moment. Of this sings a village mystic in Bengal:

> My eyes drown in the darkness of joy,
> My heart, like a lotus, closes its petals in the rapture of the dark night.

That song speaks of a joy which is deep like the blue sea, endless like the blue sky; which has the magnificence of the night, and in its limitless darkness enfolds the radiant worlds in the awfulness of peace; it is the unfathomed joy in which all sufferings are made one.

A poet of mediæval India tells us about his source of inspiration in a poem containing a question and an answer:

> Where were your songs, my bird, when you spent your nights in the nest?
> Was not all your pleasure stored therein?
> What makes you lose your heart to the sky, the sky that is limitless?

The bird answers:

> I had my pleasure while I rested within bounds.
> When I soared into the limitless, I found my songs!

To detach the individual idea from its confinement of everyday facts and to give its soaring wings the freedom of the universal: this is the function of poetry. The ambition of Macbeth, the jealousy of Othello, would be at best sensational in police court proceedings; but in Shakespeare's dramas they are carried among the flaming constellations where creation throbs with Eternal Passion, Eternal Pain.

THE RELIGION OF THE FOREST

THE RELIGION OF THE FOREST

I

We stand before this great world. The truth of our life depends upon our attitude of mind towards it—an attitude which is formed by our habit of dealing with it according to the special circumstance of our surroundings and our temperaments. It guides our attempts to establish relations with the universe either by conquest or by union, either through the cultivation of power or through that of sympathy. And thus, in our realisation of the truth of existence, we put our emphasis either upon the principle of dualism or upon the principle of unity.

The Indian sages have held in the Upanishads that the emancipation of our soul lies in its realising the ultimate truth of unity. They said:

> Isháyásyam idam sarvam yat kinch jagatyám jagat.
> Yéna tyakténa bhunjithá má graha kasyasvit dhanam.

(Know all that moves in this moving world as enveloped by God; and find enjoyment through renunciation, not through greed of possession.)

The meaning of this is, that, when we know the multiplicity of things as the final truth, we try to augment ourselves by the external possession of them; but, when we know the Infinite Soul as the final truth, then through our union with it we realise the joy of our soul. Therefore it has been said of those who have attained their fulfilment,—"sarvam evá vishanti" (they enter into all things). Their perfect relation with this world is the relation of union.

This ideal of perfection preached by the forest-dwellers of ancient India runs through the heart of our classical literature and still dominates our mind. The legends related in our epics cluster under the forest shade bearing all through their narrative the message of the forest-dwellers. Our two greatest classical dramas find their background in scenes of the forest hermitage, which are permeated by the association of these sages.

The history of the Northmen of Europe is resonant with the music of the sea. That sea is not merely topographical in its significance, but represents certain ideals of life which still guide the history and inspire the creations of that race. In the sea, nature presented herself to those men in her aspect of a danger, a barrier which seemed to be at constant war with the land and its children. The sea was the challenge of untamed nature to the indomitable human soul. And man did not flinch; he fought and won, and the spirit of fight continued in him. This fight he still maintains; it is the fight against disease and poverty, tyranny of matter and of man.

This refers to a people who live by the sea, and ride on it as on a wild, champing horse, catching it by its mane and making it render service from shore to shore. They find delight in turning by force the antagonism of circumstances into obedience. Truth appears to them in her aspect of dualism, the perpetual conflict of good and evil, which has no reconciliation, which can only end in victory or defeat.

But in the level tracts of Northern India men found no barrier between their lives and the grand life that permeates the universe. The forest entered into a close living relationship with their work and leisure, with their daily necessities and contemplations. They could not think of other surroundings as separate or inimical. So the view of the truth, which these men found, did not make manifest the difference, but rather the unity of all things. They uttered their faith in these words: "Yadidam kinch sarvam prâna éjati nihsratam" (All that is vibrates with life, having come out from life). When we know this world as alien to us, then its mechanical aspect takes prominence in our mind; and then we set up our machines and our methods to deal with it and make as much profit as our knowledge of its mechanism allows us to do. This view of things does not play us false, for the machine has its place in this world. And not only this material universe, but human beings also, may be used as machines and made to yield powerful results. This aspect of truth cannot be ignored; it has to be known and mastered. Europe has done so and has reaped a rich harvest.

The view of this world which India has taken is summed up in one compound Sanskrit word, Sachidānanda. The meaning is that Reality, which is essentially one, has three phases. The first is Sat; it is the simple fact that things are, the fact which relates us to all things through the relationship of common existence. The second is Chit; it is the fact that we know, which relates us to all things through the relationship of knowledge. The third is Ananda: it is the fact that we enjoy, which unites us with all things through the relationship of love.

According to the true Indian view, our consciousness of the world, merely as the sum total of things that exist, and as governed by laws, is imperfect. But it is perfect when our consciousness realises all things as spiritually one with it, and therefore capable of giving us joy. For us the highest purpose of this world is not merely living in it, knowing it and making use of it, but realising our own selves in it through expansion of sympathy; not alienating ourselves from it and dominating it, but comprehending and uniting it with ourselves in perfect union.

II

When Vikramâditya became king, Ujjayini a great capital, and Kâlidâsa its poet, the age of India's forest retreats had passed. Then we had taken our stand in the midst of the great concourse of humanity. The Chinese and the Hun, the Scythian and the Persian, the Greek and the Roman, had crowded round us. But, even in that age of pomp and prosperity, the love and reverence with which its poet sang about the hermitage shows what was the dominant ideal that occupied the mind of India; what was the one current of memory that continually flowed through her life.

In Kâlidâsa's drama, *Shakuntalâ*, the hermitage, which dominates the play, overshadowing the king's palace, has the same idea running through it—the recognition of the kinship of man with conscious and unconscious creation alike.

A poet of a later age, while describing a hermitage in his Kâdambari, tells us of the posture of salutation in the flowering lianas as they bow to the wind; of the sacrifice offered by the trees scattering their blossoms; of the grove resounding with the lessons chanted by the neophytes, and the verses repeated by the parrots, learnt by constantly hearing them; of the wild-fowl enjoying "vaishva-deva-bali-pinda" (the food offered to the divinity which is in all creatures); of the ducks coming up from the lake for their portion of the grass seed spread in the cottage yards to dry; and of the deer caressing with their tongues the young hermit boys. It is again the same story. The hermitage shines out, in all our ancient literature, as the place where the chasm between man and the rest of creation has been bridged.

In the Western dramas, human characters drown our attention in the vortex of their passions. Nature occasionally peeps out, but she is almost always a trespasser, who has to offer excuses, or bow apologetically and depart. But in all our dramas which still retain their fame, such as *Mrit-Shakatikâ*, *Shakuntalâ*, *Uttara-Râma-charita*, Nature stands on her own right, proving that she has her great function, to impart the peace of the eternal to human emotions.

The fury of passion in two of Shakespeare's youthful poems is exhibited in conspicuous isolation. It is snatched away, naked, from the context of the All; it has not the green earth or the blue sky around it; it is there ready to bring to our view the raging fever which is in man's desires, and not the balm of health and repose which encircles it in the universe.

Ritûsamhâra is clearly a work of Kâlidâsa's immaturity. The youthful love-song in it does not reach the sublime reticence which is in *Shakuntalâ* and *Kumâra-Sambhava*. But the tune of these voluptuous outbreaks is set to the varied harmony of Nature's symphony. The moonbeams of the summer evening, resonant with the flow of fountains, acknowledge it as a part of its own melody. In its rhythm sways the Kadamba forest, glistening in the first cool rain of the season; and the south breezes, carrying the scent of the mango blossoms, temper it with their murmur.

In the third canto of *Kumâra-Sambhava*, Madana, the God Eros, enters the forest sanctuary to set free a sudden flood of desire amid the serenity of the ascetics' meditation. But the boisterous outbreak of passion so caused was shown against a background of universal life. The divine love-thrills of Sati and Shiva found their response in the world-wide immensity of youth, in which animals and trees have their life-throbs.

Not only its third canto but the whole of the Kumâra-Sambhava poem is painted upon a limitless canvas. It tells of the eternal wedding of love, its wooing and sacrifice, and its fulfilment, for which the gods wait in suspense. Its inner idea is deep and of all time. It answers the one question that humanity asks through all its endeavours: "How is the birth of the hero to be brought about, the brave one who can defy and vanquish the evil demon laying waste heaven's own kingdom?"

It becomes evident that such a problem had become acute in Kâlidâsa's time, when the old simplicity of Hindu life had broken up. The Hindu kings, forgetful of their duties, had become self-seeking epicureans, and India was being repeatedly devastated by the Scythians.

What answer, then, does the poem give to the question it raises? Its message is that the cause of weakness lies in the inner life of the soul. It is in some break of harmony with the Good, some dissociation from the True. In the commencement of the poem we find that the God Shiva, the Good, had remained for long lost in the self-centred solitude of his asceticism, detached from the world of reality. And then Paradise was lost. But *Kumâra-Sambhava* is the poem of Paradise Regained. How was it regained? When Sati, the Spirit of Reality, through humiliation, suffering, and penance, won the Heart of Shiva, the Spirit of Goodness. And thus, from the union of the freedom of the real with the restraint of the Good, was born the heroism that released Paradise from the demon of Lawlessness.

Viewed from without, India, in the time of Kâlidâsa, appeared to have reached the zenith of civilisation, excelling as she did in luxury, literature and the arts. But from the poems of Kâlidâsa it is evident that this very magnificence of wealth and enjoyment worked against the ideal that sprang and flowed forth from the sacred solitude of the forest. These poems contain the voice of warnings against the gorgeous unreality of that age, which, like a Himalayan avalanche, was slowly gliding down to an abyss of catastrophe. And from his seat beside all the glories of Vikramâditya's throne the poet's heart yearns for the purity and simplicity of India's past age of spiritual striving. And it was this yearning which impelled him to go back to the annals of the ancient Kings of Raghu's line for the narrative poem, in which he traced the history of the rise and fall of the ideal that should guide the rulers of men.

King Dilipa, with Queen Sudakshinâ, has entered upon the life of the forest. The great monarch is busy tending the cattle of the hermitage. Thus the poem opens, amid scenes of simplicity and self-denial. But it ends in the palace of magnificence, in the extravagance of self-enjoyment. With a calm restraint of language the poet tells us of the kingly glory crowned with purity. He begins his poem as the day begins, in the serenity of sunrise. But lavish are the colours in which he describes the end, as of the evening, eloquent for a time with the sumptuous splendour of sunset, but overtaken at last by the devouring darkness which sweeps away all its brilliance into night.

In this beginning and this ending of his poem

there lies hidden that message of the forest which found its voice in the poet's words. There runs through the narrative the idea that the future glowed gloriously ahead only when there was in the atmosphere the calm of self-control, of purity and renunciation. When downfall had become imminent, the hungry fires of desire, aflame at a hundred different points, dazzled the eyes of all beholders.

Kâlidâsa in almost all his works represented the unbounded impetuousness of kingly splendour on the one side and the serene strength of regulated desires on the other. Even in the minor drama of *Mâlavikâgnimitra* we find the same thing in a different manner. It must never be thought that, in this play, the poet's deliberate object was to pander to his royal patron by inviting him to a literary orgy of lust and passion. The very introductory verse indicates the object towards which this play is directed. The poet begins the drama with the prayer, "Sanmârgâlókayan vyapanayatu sa nastâmasi vritimishah" (Let God, to illumine for us the path of truth, sweep away our passions, bred of darkness). This is the God Shiva, in whose nature Parvati, the eternal Woman, is ever commingled in an ascetic purity of love. The unified being of Shiva and Parvati is the perfect symbol of the eternal in the wedded love of man and woman. When the poet opens his drama with an invocation of this Spirit of the Divine Union it is evident that it contains in it the message with which he greets his kingly audience. The whole drama goes to show the ugliness of the treachery and cruelty inherent in unchecked self-indulgence. In the play the conflict of ideals is between the King and the Queen, between Agnimitra and Dhârini, and the significance of the contrast lies hidden in the very names of the hero and the heroine. Though the name Agnimitra is historical, yet it symbolises in the poet's mind the destructive force of uncontrolled desire—just as did the name Agnivarna in *Raghuvamsha.* Agnimitra, "the friend of the fire," the reckless person, who in his love-making is playing with fire, not knowing that all the time it is scorching him black. And what a great name is Dhârini, signifying the fortitude and forbearance that comes from majesty of soul! What an association it carries of the infinite dignity of love, purified by a self-abnegation that rises far above all insult and baseness of betrayal!

In *Shakuntalâ* this conflict of ideals has been

shown, all through the drama, by the contrast of the pompous heartlessness of the king's court and the natural purity of the forest hermitage. The drama opens with a hunting scene, where the king is in pursuit of an antelope. The cruelty of the chase appears like a menace symbolising the spirit of the king's life clashing against the spirit of the forest retreat, which is "sharanyam sarva-bhútânâm" (where all creatures find their protection of love). And the pleading of the forest-dwellers with the king to spare the life of the deer, helplessly innocent and beautiful, is the pleading that rises from the heart of the whole drama. "Never, oh, never is the arrow meant to pierce the tender body of a deer, even as the fire is not for the burning of flowers."

In the *Râmâyana*, Rama and his companions, in their banishment, had to traverse forest after forest; they had to live in leaf-thatched huts, to sleep on the bare ground. But as their hearts felt their kinship with woodland, hill, and stream, they were not in exile amidst these. Poets, brought up in an atmosphere of different ideals, would have taken this opportunity of depicting in dismal colours the hardship of the forest-life in order to bring out the martyrdom of Râmachandra with all the emphasis of a strong contrast. But, in the *Râmâyana*, we are led to realise the greatness of the hero, not in a fierce struggle with Nature, but in sympathy with it. Sitâ, the daughter-in-law of a great kingly house, goes along the forest paths. We read:

"She asks Râma about the flowering trees, and shrubs and creepers which she has not seen before. At her request Lakshmana gathers and brings her plants of all kinds, exuberant with flowers, and it delights her heart to see the forest rivers, variegated with their streams and sandy banks, resounding with the call of heron and duck.

"When Râma first took his abode in the Chitrakuta peak, that delightful Chitrakuta, by the Mâlyavati river, with its easy slopes for landing, he forgot all the pain of leaving his home in the capital at the sight of those woodlands, alive with beast and bird."

Having lived on that hill for long, Râma, who was "giri-vana-priya" (lover of the mountain and the forest), said one day to Sitâ:

"When I look upon the beauties of this hill, the loss of my kingdom troubles me no longer, nor does the separation from my friends cause me any pang."

Thus passed Râmachandra's exile, now in woodland, now in hermitage. The love which Râma and Sitâ bore to each other united them, not only to each other, but to the universe of life. That is why, when Sitâ was taken away, the loss seemed to be so great to the forest itself.

III

Strangely enough, in Shakespeare's dramas, like those of Kâlidâsa, we find a secret vein of complaint against the artificial life of the king's court—the life of ungrateful treachery and falsehood. And almost everywhere, in his dramas, foreign scenes have been introduced in connection with some working of the life of unscrupulous ambition. It is perfectly obvious in *Timon of Athens*—but there Nature offers no message or balm to the injured soul of man. In *Cymbeline* the mountainous forest and the cave appear in their aspect of obstruction to life's opportunities. These only seem tolerable in comparison with the vicissitudes of fortune in the artificial court life. In *As You Like It* the forest of Arden is didactic in its lessons. It does not bring peace, but preaches, when it says:

Hath not old custom made this life more sweet
Than that of painted pomp? Are not these woods
More free from peril than the envious court?

In the *Tempest*, through Prospero's treatment of Ariel and Caliban we realise man's struggle with Nature and his longing to sever connection with her. In *Macbeth*, as a prelude to a bloody crime of treachery and treason, we are introduced to a scene of barren heath where the three witches appear as personifications of Nature's malignant forces; and in *King Lear* it is the fury of a father's love turned into curses by the ingratitude born of the unnatural life of the court that finds its symbol in the storm on the heath. The tragic intensity of *Hamlet* and *Othello* is unrelieved by any touch of Nature's eternity. Except in a passing glimpse of a moonlight night in the love scene in the *Merchant of Venice*, Nature has not been allowed in other dramas of this series, including *Romeo and Juliet* and *Antony and Cleopatra*, to contribute her own music to the music of man's love. In *The Winter's Tale* the cruelty of a king's suspicion stands bare in its relentlessness, and Nature cowers before it, offering no consolation.

I hope it is needless for me to say that these

observations are not intended to minimise Shakespeare's great power as a dramatic poet, but to show in his works the gulf between Nature and human nature owing to the tradition of his race and time. It cannot be said that beauty of nature is ignored in his writings; only he fails to recognise in them the truth of the interpenetration of human life with the cosmic life of the world. We observe a completely different attitude of mind in the later English poets like Wordsworth and Shelley, which can be attributed in the main to the great mental change in Europe, at that particular period, through the influence of the newly discovered philosophy of India which stirred the soul of Germany and aroused the attention of other Western countries.

In Milton's *Paradise Lost*, the very subject—Man dwelling in the garden of Paradise—seems to afford a special opportunity for bringing out the true greatness of man's relationship with Nature. But though the poet has described to us the beauties of the garden, though he has shown to us the animals living there in amity and peace among themselves, there is no reality of kinship between them and man. They were created for man's enjoyment; man was their lord and master. We find no trace of the love between the first man and woman gradually surpassing themselves and overflowing the rest of creation, such as we find in the love scenes in *Kumâra-Sambhava* and *Shakuntalâ.* In the seclusion of the bower, where the first man and woman rested in the garden of Paradise—

> Bird, beast, insect or worm
> Durst enter none, such was their awe of man.

Not that India denied the superiority of man, but the test of that superiority lay, according to her, in the comprehensiveness of sympathy, not in the aloofness of absolute distinction.

IV

India holds sacred, and counts as places of pilgrimage, all spots which display a special beauty or splendour of nature. These had no original attraction on account of any special fitness for cultivation or settlement. Here, man is free, not to look upon Nature as a source of supply of his necessities, but to realise his soul beyond himself. The Himâlayas of India are sacred and the Vindhya Hills. Her majestic rivers are sacred. Lake Mânasa and the confluence of the Ganges and the Jamuna are sacred. India has saturated with her love and worship the great Nature with which her children are surrounded, whose light fills their eyes with gladness, and whose water cleanses them, whose food gives them life, and from whose majestic mystery comes forth the constant revelation of the infinite in music, scent, and colour, which brings its awakening to the soul of man. India gains the world through worship, through spiritual communion; and the idea of freedom to which she aspired was based upon the realisation of her spiritual unity.

When, in my recent voyage to Europe, our ship left Aden and sailed along the sea which lay between the two continents, we passed by the red and barren rocks of Arabia on our right side and the gleaming sands of Egypt on our left. They seemed to me like two giant brothers exchanging with each other burning glances of hatred, kept apart by the tearful entreaty of the sea from whose womb they had their birth.

There was an immense stretch of silence on the left shore as well as on the right, but the two shores spoke to me of the two different historical dramas enacted. The civilisation which found its growth in Egypt was continued across long centuries, elaborately rich with sentiments and expressions of life, with pictures, sculptures, temples, and ceremonials. This was a country whose guardian-spirit was a noble river, which spread the festivities of life on its banks across the heart of the land. There man never raised the barrier of alienation between himself and the rest of the world.

On the opposite shore of the Red Sea the civilisation which grew up in the inhospitable soil of Arabia had a contrary character to that of Egypt. There man felt himself isolated in his hostile and bare surroundings. His idea of God became that of a jealous God. His mind naturally dwelt upon the principle of separateness. It roused in him the spirit of fight, and this spirit was a force that drove him far and wide. These two civilisations represented two fundamental divisions of human nature. The one contained in it the spirit of conquest and the other the spirit of harmony. And both of these have their truth and purpose in human existence.

The characters of two eminent sages have been described in our mythology. One was Vashishtha and another Vishvâmitra. Both of them were great, but they represented two different types of wisdom; and there was conflict between them. Vishvâmitra sought to achieve power and was proud of it; Vashishtha was rudely smitten by that power. But his hurt and his loss could not touch the illumination of his soul; for he rose above them and could forgive. Râmachandra, the great hero of our epic, had his initiation to the spiritual life from Vashishtha, the life of inner peace and perfection. But he had his initiation to war from Vishvâmitra, who called him to kill the demons and gave him weapons that were irresistible.

Those two sages symbolise in themselves the two guiding spirits of civilisation. Can it be true that they shall never be reconciled? If so, can ever the age of peace and co-operation dawn upon the human world? Creation is the harmony of contrary forces—the forces of attraction and repulsion. When they join hands, all the fire and fight are changed into the smile of flowers and the songs of birds. When there is only one of them triumphant and the other defeated, then either there is the death of cold rigidity or that of suicidal explosion.

Humanity, for ages, has been busy with the one great creation of spiritual life. Its best wisdom, its discipline, its literature and art, all the teachings and self-sacrifice of its noblest teachers, have been for this. But the harmony of contrary forces, which give their rhythm to all creation, has not yet been perfected by man in his civilisation, and the Creator in him is baffled over and over again. He comes back to his work, however, and makes himself busy, building his world in the midst of desolation and ruins. His history is the history of his aspiration interrupted and renewed. And one truth of which he must be reminded, therefore, is that the power which accomplishes the miracle of creation, by bringing conflicting forces into the harmony of the One, is no passion, but a love which accepts the bonds of self-control from the joy of its own immensity—a love whose sacrifice is the manifestation of its endless wealth within itself.

AN INDIAN FOLK RELIGION

AN INDIAN FOLK RELIGION

I

In historical time the Buddha comes first of those who declared salvation to all men, without distinction, as by right man's own. What was the special force which startled men's minds and, almost within the master's lifetime, spread his teachings over India? It was the unique significance of the event, when a man came to men and said to them, "I am here to emancipate you from the miseries of the thraldom of self." This wisdom came, neither in texts of Scripture, nor in symbols of deities, nor in religious practices sanctified by ages, but through the voice of a living man and the love that flowed from a human heart.

And I believe this was the first occasion in the history of the world when the idea of the Avatâr found its place in religion. Western scholars are never tired of insisting that Buddhism is of the nature of a moral code, coldly leading to the path of extinction. They forget that it was held to be a religion that roused in its devotees an inextinguishable fire of enthusiasm and carried them to lifelong exile across the mountain and desert barriers. To say that a philosophy of suicide can keep kindled in human hearts for centuries such fervour of self-sacrifice is to go against all the laws of sane psychology. The religious enthusiasm which cannot be bound within any daily ritual, but overflows into adventures of love and beneficence, must have in its centre that element of personality which rouses the whole soul. In answer, it may possibly be said that this was due to the personality of Buddha himself. But that also is not quite true. The personality which stirs the human heart to its immense depths, leading it to impossible deeds of heroism, must in that process itself reveal to men the infinite which is in all humanity. And that is what happened in Buddhism, making it a religion in the complete sense of the word.

Like the religion of the Upanishads, Buddhism also generated two divergent currents; the one impersonal, preaching the abnegation of self through discipline, and the other personal, preaching the cultivation of sympathy for all creatures, and devotion to the infinite truth of love; the other, which is called the Mahâyâna, had its origin in the positive element contained in Buddha's teachings, which is immeasurable love. It could never, by any logic, find its reality in the emptiness of the truthless abyss. And the object of Buddha's meditation and his teachings was to free humanity from sufferings. But what was the path that he revealed to us? Was it some negative way of evading pain and seeking security against it? On the contrary, his path was the path of sacrifice—the utmost sacrifice of love. The meaning of such sacrifice is to reach some ultimate truth, some positive ideal, which in its greatness can accept suffering and transmute it into the profound peace of self-renunciation. True emancipation from suffering, which is the inalienable condition of the limited life of the self, can never be attained by fleeing from it, but rather by changing its value in the realm of truth—the truth of the higher life of love.

We have learnt that, by calculations made in accordance with the law of gravitation, some planets were discovered exactly in the place where they should be. Such a law of gravitation there is also in the moral world. And when we find men's minds disturbed, as they were by the preaching of the Buddha, we can be sure, even without any corroborative evidence, that there must have been some great luminous body of attraction, positive and powerful, and not a mere unfathomable vacancy. It is exactly this which we discover in the heart of the Mahâyâna system; and we have no hesitation in saying that the truth of Buddhism is there. The oil has to be burnt, not for the purpose of diminishing it, but for the purpose of giving light to the lamp. And when the Buddha said that the self must go, he said at the same moment that love must be realised. Thus originated the doctrine of the Dharma-kâya, the Infinite Wisdom and Love manifested in the Buddha. It was the first instance, as I have said, when men felt that the Universal and the Eternal Spirit was revealed in a human individual whom they had known and touched. The joy was too great for them, since the very idea itself came to them as a freedom—a freedom from the sense of their measureless insignificance. It was the first time, I repeat, when the individual, as a man, felt in himself the Infinite made concrete.

What was more, those men who felt the love welling forth from the heart of Buddhism, as one with the current of the Eternal Love itself, were struck with the idea that such an effluence could never have been due to a single cataclysm of history—unnatural and therefore untrue. They felt instead that it was in the eternal nature of truth, that the event must belong to a series of manifestations; there must have been numberless other revelations in the past and endless others to follow.

The idea grew and widened until men began to feel that this Infinite Being was already in every one of them, and that it rested with themselves to remove the sensual obstructions and reveal him in their own lives. In every individual there was, they realised, the potentiality of Buddha—that is to say, the Infinite made manifest.

We have to keep in mind the great fact that the preaching of the Buddha in India was not followed by stagnation of life—as would surely have happened if humanity was without any positive goal and his teaching was without any permanent value in itself. On the contrary, we find the arts and sciences springing up in its wake, institutions started for alleviating the misery of all creatures, human and non-human, and great centres of education founded. Some mighty power was suddenly roused from its obscurity, which worked for long centuries and changed the history of man in a large part of the world. And that power came into its full activity only by the individual being made conscious of his infinite worth. It was like the sudden discovery of a great mine of living wealth.

During the period of Buddhism the doctrine of deliverance flourished, which reached all mankind and released man's inner resources from neglect and self-insult. Even to-day we see in our own country human nature, from its despised corner of indignity, slowly and painfully finding its way to assert the inborn majesty of man. It is like the imprisoned tree finding a rift in the wall, and sending out its eager branches into freedom, to prove that darkness is not its birthright, that its love is for the sunshine. In the time of the Buddha the individual discovered his own immensity of worth, first by witnessing a man who united his heart in sympathy with all creatures, in all worlds, through the power of a love that knew no bounds; and then by learning that the same light of perfection lay confined within himself behind the clouds of selfish desire, and that the Bodhi-hridaya—"the heart of the Eternal Enlightenment"—every moment claimed its unveiling in his own heart. Nâgârjuna speaks of this Bodhi-hridaya (another of whose names is Bodhi-Citta) as follows:

> One who understands the nature of the Bodhi-hridaya, sees everything with a loving heart; for love is the essence of Bodhi-hridaya.[1]

My object in writing this paper is to show, by the further help of illustration from a popular religious sect of Bengal, that the religious instinct of man urges him towards a truth, by which he can transcend the finite nature of the individual self. Man would never feel the indignity of his limitations if these were inevitable. Within him he has glimpses of the Infinite, which give him assurance that this truth is not in his limitations, but that this truth can be attained by love. For love is the positive quality of the Infinite, and love's sacrifice accordingly does not lead to emptiness, but to fulfilment, to Bodhi-hridaya, "the heart of enlightenment."

The members of the religious sect I have

[1] *Outlines of Mahâyâna Buddhism*, by Dr. D. T. Suzaki.

mentioned call themselves "Baül." They live outside social recognition, and their very obscurity helps them in their seeking, from a direct source, the enlightenment which the soul longs for, the eternal light of love.

It would be absurd to say that there is little difference between Buddhism and the religion of these simple people, who have no system of metaphysics to support their faith. But my object in bringing close together these two religions, which seem to belong to opposite poles, is to point out the fundamental unity in them. Both of them believe in a fulfilment which is reached by love's emancipating us from the dominance of self. In both these religions we find man's yearning to attain the infinite worth of his individuality, not through any conventional valuation of society, but through his perfect relationship with Truth. They agree in holding that the realisation of our ultimate object is waiting for us in ourselves. The Baül likens this fulfilment to the blossoming of a bud, and sings:

> Make way, O bud, make way,
>   Burst open thy heart and make way.
> The opening spirit has overtaken thee,
>   Canst thou remain a bud any longer?

II

One day, in a small village in Bengal, an ascetic woman from the neighbourhood came to see me. She had the name "Sarva-khepi" given to her by the village people, the meaning of which is "the woman who is mad about all things." She fixed her star-like eyes upon my face and startled me with the question, "When are you coming to meet me underneath the trees?" Evidently she pitied me who lived (according to her) prisoned behind walls, banished away from the great meeting-place of the All, where she had her dwelling. Just at that moment my gardener came with his basket, and when the woman understood that the flowers in the vase on my table were going to be thrown away, to make place for the fresh ones, she looked pained and said to me, "You are always engaged reading and writing; you do not see." Then she took the discarded flowers in her palms, kissed them and touched them with her forehead, and reverently murmured to herself, "Beloved of my heart." I felt that this woman, in her direct vision of the infinite personality in the heart of all things, truly represented the spirit of India.

In the same village I came into touch with some Baül singers. I had known them by their names, occasionally seen them singing and begging in the street, and so passed them by, vaguely classifying them in my mind under the general name of Vairâgis, or ascetics.

The time came when I had occasion to meet with some members of the same body and talk to them about spiritual matters. The first Baül song, which I chanced to hear with any attention, profoundly stirred my mind. Its words are so simple that it makes me hesitate to render them in a foreign tongue, and set them forward for critical observation. Besides, the best part of a song is missed when the tune is absent; for thereby its movement and its colour are lost, and it becomes like a butterfly whose wings have been plucked.

The first line may be translated thus: "Where shall I meet him, the Man of my Heart?" This phrase, "the Man of my Heart," is not peculiar to this song, but is usual with the Baül sect. It means that, for me, the supreme truth of all existence is in the revelation of the Infinite in my own humanity.

"The Man of my Heart," to the Baül, is like a divine instrument perfectly tuned. He gives expression to infinite truth in the music of life. And the longing for the truth which is in us, which we have not yet realised, breaks out in the following Baül song:

> Where shall I meet him, the Man of my Heart?
> He is lost to me and I seek him wandering from land to land.
>
> I am listless for that moonrise of beauty,
> which is to light my life,
> which I long to see in the fulness of vision, in gladness of heart.

The name of the poet who wrote this song was Gagan. He was almost illiterate; and the ideas he received from his Baül teacher found no distraction from the self-consciousness of the modern age. He was a village postman, earning about ten shillings a month, and he died before he had completed his teens. The sentiment, to which he gave such intensity of expression, is common to most of the songs of his sect. And it is a sect, almost exclusively confined to that lower floor of society, where the light of modern education hardly finds an entrance, while wealth and respectability shun its utter indigence.

In the song I have translated above, the longing of the singer to realise the infinite in his own personality is expressed. This has to be done daily by its perfect expression in life, in love. For the personal expression of life, in its perfection, is love; just as the personal expression of truth in its perfection is beauty.

In the political life of the modern age the idea of democracy has given mankind faith in the individual. It gives each man trust in his own possibilities, and pride in his humanity. Something of the same idea, we find, has been working in the popular mind of India, with regard to its religious consciousness. Over and over again it tries to assert, not only that God is *for* each of us, but also that God is *in* each of us. These people have no special incarnations in their simple theology, because they know that God is special to each individual. They say that to be born a man is the greatest privilege that can fall to a creature in all the world. They assert that gods in Paradise envy human beings. Why? Because God's will, in giving his love, finds its completeness in man's will returning that love. Therefore Humanity is a necessary factor in the perfecting of the divine truth. The Infinite, for its self-expression, comes down into the manifoldness of the Finite; and the Finite, for its self-realisation, must rise into the unity of the Infinite. Then only is the Cycle of Truth complete.

The dignity of man, in his eternal right of Truth, finds expression in the following song, composed, not by a theologian or a man of letters, but by one who belongs to that ninety per cent of the population of British India whose education has been far less than elementary, in fact almost below zero:

> My longing is to meet you in play of love, my Lover;
> But this longing is not only mine, but also yours.
> For your lips can have their smile, and your flute
>   its music, only in your delight in my love;
>   and therefore you are importunate, even as I am.

If the world were a mere expression of formative forces, then this song would be pathetic in its presumption. But why is there beauty at all in creation—the beauty whose only meaning is in a call that claims disinterestedness as a response? The poet proudly says: "Your flute could not have its music of beauty if your delight were not in my love. Your power is great—and there I am not equal to you—but it lies even in me to make you smile, and if you and I never meet, then this play of love remains incomplete."

If this were not true, then it would be an utter humiliation to exist at all in this world. If it were solely *our* business to seek the

Lover, and *his* to keep himself passively aloof in the infinity of his glory, or actively masterful only in imposing his commands upon us, then we should dare to defy him, and refuse to accept the everlasting insult latent in the one-sided importunity of a slave. And this is what the Baül says—he who, in the world of men, goes about singing for alms from door to door, with his one-stringed instrument and long robe of patched-up rags on his back:

> I stop and sit here on the road. Do not ask me to walk farther.
> If your love can be complete without mine, let me turn back from seeing you.
> I have been travelling to seek you, my friend, for long;
> Yet I refuse to beg a sight of you, if you do not feel my need.
> I am blind with market dust and midday glare,
> and so wait, my heart's lover, in hopes that your own love will send you to find me out.

The poet is fully conscious that his value in the world's market is pitifully small; that he is neither wealthy nor learned. Yet he has his great compensation, for he has come close to his Lover's heart. In Bengal the women bathing in the river often use their overturned water jars to keep themselves floating when they swim, and the poet uses this incident for his simile:

It is lucky that I am an empty vessel,
For when you swim, I keep floating by your side.
Your full vessels are left on the empty shore, they are for use;
But I am carried to the river in your arms, and I dance to the rhythm of your heart-throbs and heaving of the waves.

The great distinguished people of the world do not know that these beggars—deprived of education, honour, and wealth—can, in the pride of their souls, look down upon them as the unfortunate ones, who are left on the shore for their worldly uses, but whose life ever misses the touch of the Lover's arms.

The feeling that man is not a mere casual visitor at the palace-gate of the world, but the invited guest whose presence is needed to give the royal banquet its sole meaning, is not confined to any particular sect in India. Let me quote here some poems from a mediæval poet of Western India—Jnândâs—whose works are nearly forgotten, and have become scarce from the very exquisiteness of their excellence. In the following poem he is addressing God's messenger, who comes to us in the morning light of our childhood, in the dusk of our day's end, and in the night's darkness:

Messenger, morning brought you, habited in gold.
After sunset, your song wore a tune of ascetic grey,
and then came night.
Your message was written in bright letters across the black.
Why is such splendour about you, to lure the heart of one
who is nothing?

This is the answer of the messenger:

Great is the festival hall where you are to be the only guest.
Therefore the letter to you is written from sky to sky,
And I, the proud servant, bring the invitation with all
ceremony.

And thus the poet knows that the silent rows of stars carry God's own invitation to the individual soul.

The same poet sings:

What hast thou come to beg from the beggar, O King of
Kings?
My Kingdom is poor for want of him, my dear one, and I
wait for him in sorrow.
How long will you keep him waiting, O wretch,
who has waited for you for ages in silence and stillness?
Open your gate, and make this very moment fit for the union.

It is the song of man's pride in the value given to him by Supreme Love and realised by his own love.

The Vaishnava religion, which has become the popular religion of India, carries the same message: God's love finding its finality in man's love. According to it, the lover, man, is the complement of the Lover, God, in the internal love drama of existence; and God's call is ever wafted in man's heart in the world-music, drawing him towards the union. This idea has been expressed in rich elaboration of symbols verging upon realism. But for these Baüls this idea is direct and simple, full of the dignified beauty of truth, which shuns all tinsels of ornament.

The Baül poet, when asked why he had no sect mark on his forehead, answered in his song that the true colour decoration appears on the skin of the fruit when its inner core is filled with ripe, sweet juice; but by artificially smearing it with colour from outside you do not make it ripe. And he says of his Guru, his teacher, that he is puzzled to find in which direction he must make salutation. For his teacher is not one, but many, who, moving on, form a procession of wayfarers.

Baüls have no temple or image for their worship, and this utter simplicity is needful for men whose one subject is to realise the innermost nearness of God. The Baül poet expressly says that if we try to approach God through the senses we miss him:

> Bring him not into your house as the guest of your eyes;
>   but let him come at your heart's invitation.
> Opening your doors to that which is seen only, is to lose it.

Yet, being a poet, he also knows that the objects of sense can reveal their spiritual meaning only when they are not seen through mere physical eyes:

Eyes can see only dust and earth,
But feel it with your heart, it is pure joy.
The flowers of delight blossom on all sides, in every form,
but where is your heart's thread to weave them in a garland?

These Baüls have a philosophy, which they call the philosophy of the body; but they keep its secret; it is only for the initiated. Evidently the underlying idea is that the individual's body is itself the temple, in whose inner mystic shrine the Divine appears before the soul, and the key to it has to be found from those who know. But as the key is not for us outsiders, I leave it with the observation that this mystic philosophy of the body is the outcome of the attempt to get rid of all the outward shelters which are too costly for people like themselves. But this human body of ours is made by God's own hand, from his own love, and even if some men, in the pride of their superiority, may despise it, God finds his joy in dwelling in others of yet lower birth. It is a truth easier of discovery by these people of humble origin than by men of proud estate.

The pride of the Baül beggar is not in his worldly distinction, but in the distinction that God himself has given to him. He feels himself like a flute through which God's own breath of love has been breathed:

My heart is like a flute he has played on.
If ever it fall into other hands,—
let him fling it away.
My lover's flute is dear to him.
Therefore, if to-day alien breath have entered it and sounded strange notes,
Let him break it to pieces and strew the dust with them.

So we find that this man also has his disgust of defilement. While the ambitious world of wealth and power despises him, he in his turn thinks that the world's touch desecrates him who has been made sacred by the touch of his Lover. He does not envy us our life of ambition and achievements, but he knows how precious his own life has been:

I am poured forth in living notes of joy and sorrow by your breath.
Morning and evening, in summer and in rains, I am fashioned to music.
Yet should I be wholly spent in some flight of song,
I shall not grieve, the tune is so precious to me.

Our joys and sorrows are contradictory when self separates them in opposition. But for the heart in which self merges in God's love, they lose their absoluteness. So the Baül's prayer is to feel in all situations—in danger, or pain, or sorrow—that he is in God's hands. He solves the problem of emancipation from sufferings by accepting and setting them in a higher context:

I am the boat, you are the sea, and also the boatman.
Though you never make the shore, though you let me sink, why should I be foolish and afraid?
Is the reaching the shore a greater prize than losing myself with you?
If you are only the haven, as they say, then what is the sea?
Let it surge and toss me on its waves, I shall be content.
I live in you, whatever and however you appear.
Save me or kill me as you wish, only never leave me in others' hands.

III

It is needless to say, before I conclude, that I had neither the training nor the opportunity to study this mendicant religious sect in Bengal from an ethnological standpoint. I was attracted to find out how the living currents of religious movements work in the heart of the people, saving them from degradation imposed by the society of the learned, of the rich, or of the high-born; how the spirit of man, by making use even of its obstacles, reaches fulfilment, led thither, not by the learned authorities in the scriptures, or by the mechanical impulse of the dogma-driven crowd, but by the unsophisticated aspiration of the loving soul. On the inaccessible mountain peaks of theology the snows of creed remain eternally rigid, cold, and pure. But God's manifest shower falls direct on the plain of humble hearts, flowing there in various channels, even getting mixed with some mud in its course, as it is soaked into the underground currents, invisible, but ever-moving.

I can think of nothing better than to conclude my paper with a poem of Jnândâs, in which the aspiration of all simple spirits has found a devout expression:

I had travelled all day and was tired; then I bowed my head
towards thy kingly court still far away.
The night deepened, a longing burned in my heart.
Whatever the words I sang, pain cried through them—for
even my songs thirsted—
O my Lover, my Beloved, my Best in all the world.

When time seemed lost in darkness,
thy hand dropped its sceptre to take up the lute and
strike the uttermost chords;
And my heart sang out,
O my Lover, my Beloved, my Best in all the world.

Ah, who is this whose arms enfold me?
Whatever I have to leave, let me leave; and whatever I
have to bear, let me bear.
Only let me walk with thee,
O my Lover, my Beloved, my Best in all the world.

Descend at whiles from thy high audience hall, come down
amid joys and sorrows.
Hide in all forms and delights, in love,
And in my heart sing thy songs,—
O my Lover, my Beloved, my Best in all the world.

EAST AND WEST

EAST AND WEST

I

It is not always a profound interest in man that carries travellers nowadays to distant lands. More often it is the facility for rapid movement. For lack of time and for the sake of convenience we generalise and crush our human facts into the packages within the steel trunks that hold our travellers' reports.

Our knowledge of our own countrymen and our feelings about them have slowly and unconsciously grown out of innumerable facts which are full of contradictions and subject to incessant change. They have the elusive mystery and fluidity of life. We cannot define to ourselves what we are as a whole, because we know too much; because our knowledge is more than knowledge. It is an immediate consciousness of personality, any evaluation of which carries some emotion, joy or sorrow, shame or exaltation.

But in a foreign land we try to find our compensation for the meagreness of our data by the compactness of the generalisation which our imperfect sympathy itself helps us to form. When a stranger from the West travels in the Eastern world he takes the facts that displease him and readily makes use of them for his rigid conclusions, fixed upon the unchallengeable authority of his personal experience. It is like a man who has his own boat for crossing his village stream, but, on being compelled to wade across some strange watercourse, draws angry comparisons as he goes from every patch of mud and every pebble which his feet encounter.

Our mind has faculties which are universal, but its habits are insular. There are men who become impatient and angry at the least discomfort when their habits are incommoded. In their idea of the next world they probably conjure up the ghosts of their slippers and dressing-gowns, and expect the latchkey that opens their lodging-house door on earth to fit their front door in the other world. As travellers they are a failure; for they have grown too accustomed to their mental easy-chairs, and in their intellectual nature love home comforts, which are of local make, more than the realities of life, which, like earth itself, are full of ups and downs, yet are one in their rounded completeness.

The modern age has brought the geography of the earth near to us, but made it difficult for us to come into touch with man. We go to strange lands and observe; we do not live there. We hardly meet men: but only specimens of knowledge. We are in haste to seek for general types and overlook individuals.

When we fall into the habit of neglecting to use the understanding that comes of sympathy in our travels, our knowledge of foreign people grows insensitive, and therefore easily becomes both unjust and cruel in its character, and also selfish and contemptuous in its application. Such has, too often, been the case with regard to the meeting of Western people in our days with others for whom they do not recognise any obligation of kinship.

It has been admitted that the dealings between different races of men are not merely between individuals; that our mutual understanding is either aided, or else obstructed, by the general emanations forming the social atmosphere. These emanations are our collective ideas and collective feelings, generated according to special historical circumstances.

For instance, the caste-idea is a collective idea in India. When we approach an Indian who is under the influence of this collective idea, he is no longer a pure individual with his conscience fully awake to the judging of the value of a human being. He is more or less a passive medium for giving expression to the sentiment of a whole community.

It is evident that the caste-idea is not creative; it is merely institutional. It adjusts human beings according to some mechanical arrangement. It emphasises the negative side of the individual — his separateness. It hurts the complete truth in man.

In the West, also, the people have a certain collective idea that obscures their humanity. Let me try to explain what I feel about it.

II

Lately I went to visit some battlefields of France which had been devastated by war. The awful calm of desolation, which still bore wrinkles of pain—death-struggles stiffened into ugly ridges—brought before my mind the vision of a huge demon, which had no shape, no meaning, yet had two arms that could strike and break and tear, a gaping mouth that could devour, and bulging brains that could conspire and plan. It was a purpose, which had a living body, but no complete humanity to temper it. Because it was passion—belonging to life, and yet not having the wholeness of life—it was the most terrible of life's enemies.

Something of the same sense of oppression in a different degree, the same desolation in a different aspect, is produced in my mind when I realise the effect of the West upon Eastern life—the West which, in its relation to us, is all plan and purpose incarnate, without any superfluous humanity.

I feel the contrast very strongly in Japan. In that country the old world presents itself with some ideal of perfection, in which man has his varied opportunities of self-revelation in art, in ceremonial, in religious faith, and in customs expressing the poetry of social relationship. There one feels that deep delight of hospitality which life offers to life. And side by side, in the same soil, stands the modern world, which is stupendously big and powerful, but inhospitable. It has no simple-hearted welcome for man. It is living; yet the incompleteness of life's ideal within it cannot but hurt humanity.

The wriggling tentacles of a cold-blooded utilitarianism, with which the West has grasped all the easily yielding succulent portions of the East, are causing pain and indignation throughout the Eastern countries. The West comes to us, not with the imagination and sympathy that create and unite, but with a shock of passion—passion for power and wealth. This passion is a mere force, which has in it the principle of separation, of conflict.

I have been fortunate in coming into close touch with individual men and women of the Western countries, and have felt with them their sorrows and shared their aspirations. I have known that they seek the same God, who is my God—even those who deny Him. I feel certain that, if the great light of culture be extinct in Europe, our horizon in the East will mourn in darkness. It does not hurt my pride to acknowledge that, in the present age, Western humanity has received its mission to be the teacher of the world; that her science, through the mastery of laws of nature, is to liberate human souls from the dark dungeon of matter. For this very reason I have realised all the more strongly, on the other hand, that the dominant collective idea in the Western countries is not creative. It is ready to enslave or kill individuals, to drug a great people with soul-killing poison, darkening their whole future with the black mist of stupefaction, and emasculating entire races of men to the utmost degree of helplessness. It is wholly wanting in spiritual power to blend and harmonise; it lacks the sense of the great personality of man.

The most significant fact of modern days is this, that the West has met the East. Such a momentous meeting of humanity, in order to be fruitful, must have in its heart some great emotional idea, generous and creative. There can be no doubt that God's choice has fallen upon the knights-errant of the West for the service of the present age; arms and armour have been given to them; but have they yet realised in their hearts the single-minded loyalty to their cause which can resist all temptations of bribery from the devil? The world to-day is offered to the West. She will destroy it, if she does not use it for a great creation of man. The materials for such a creation are in the hands of science; but the creative genius is in Man's spiritual ideal.

III

When I was young a stranger from Europe came to Bengal. He chose his lodging among the people of the country, shared with them their frugal diet, and freely offered them his service. He found employment in the houses of the rich, teaching them French and German, and the money thus earned he spent to help poor students in buying books. This meant for him hours of walking in the mid-day heat of a tropical summer; for, intent upon exercising the utmost economy, he refused to hire conveyances. He was pitiless in his exaction from himself of his resources, in money, time, and strength, to the point of privation; and all this for the sake of a people who were obscure, to whom he was not born, yet whom he dearly loved. He did not come to us with a professional mission of teaching sectarian creeds; he had not in his nature the least trace of that self-sufficiency of goodness, which humiliates by gifts the victims of its insolent benevolence. Though he did not know our language, he took every occasion to frequent our meetings and ceremonies; yet he was always afraid of intrusion, and tenderly anxious lest he might offend us by his ignorance of our customs. At last, under the continual strain of work in an alien climate and surroundings, his health broke down. He died, and was cremated at our burning-ground, according to his express desire.

The attitude of his mind, the manner of his living, the object of his life, his modesty, his unstinted self-sacrifice for a people who had not even the power to give publicity to any benefaction bestowed upon them, were so utterly unlike anything we were accustomed to associate with the Europeans in India, that it gave rise in our mind to a feeling of love bordering upon awe.

We all have a realm, a private paradise, in our mind, where dwell deathless memories of persons who brought some divine light to our life's experience, who may not be known to others, and whose names have no place in the pages of history. Let me confess to you that this man lives as one of those immortals in the paradise of my individual life.

He came from Sweden, his name was Hammargren. What was most remarkable in the event of his coming to us in Bengal was the fact that in his own country he had chanced to read some works of my great countryman, Ram

Mohan Roy, and felt an immense veneration for his genius and his character. Ram Mohan Roy lived in the beginning of the last century, and it is no exaggeration when I describe him as one of the immortal personalities of modern time. This young Swede had the unusual gift of a far-sighted intellect and sympathy, which enabled him even from his distance of space and time, and in spite of racial differences, to realise the greatness of Ram Mohan Roy. It moved him so deeply that he resolved to go to the country which produced this great man, and offer her his service. He was poor, and he had to wait some time in England before he could earn his passage money to India. There he came at last, and in reckless generosity of love utterly spent himself to the last breath of his life, away from home and kindred and all the inheritances of his motherland. His stay among us was too short to produce any outward result. He failed even to achieve during his life what he had in his mind, which was to found by the help of his scanty earnings a library as a memorial to Ram Mohan Roy, and thus to leave behind him a visible symbol of his devotion. But what I prize most in this European youth, who left no record of his life behind him, is not the memory of any service of goodwill, but the precious gift of respect which he offered to a people who are fallen upon evil times, and whom it is so easy to ignore or to humiliate. For the first time in the modern days this obscure individual from Sweden brought to our country the chivalrous courtesy of the West, a greeting of human fellowship.

The coincidence came to me with a great and delightful surprise when the Nobel Prize was offered to me from Sweden. As a recognition of individual merit it was of great value to me, no doubt; but it was the acknowledgment of the East as a collaborator with the Western continents, in contributing its riches to the common stock of civilisation, which had the chief significance for the present age. It meant joining hands in comradeship by the two great hemispheres of the human world across the sea.

IV

To-day the real East remains unexplored. The blindness of contempt is more hopeless than the blindness of ignorance; for contempt kills the light which ignorance merely leaves unignited. The East is waiting to be understood by the Western races, in order not only to be able to give what is true in her, but also to be confident of her own mission.

In Indian history, the meeting of the Mussulman and the Hindu produced Akbar, the object of whose dream was the unification of hearts and ideals. It had all the glowing enthusiasm of a religion, and it produced an immediate and a vast result even in his own lifetime.

But the fact still remains that the Western mind, after centuries of contact with the East, has not evolved the enthusiasm of a chivalrous ideal which can bring this age to its fulfilment. It is everywhere raising thorny hedges of exclusion and offering human sacrifices to national self-seeking. It has intensified the mutual feelings of envy among Western races themselves, as they fight over their spoils and display a carnivorous pride in their snarling rows of teeth.

We must again guard our minds from any encroaching distrust of the individuals of a nation. The active love of humanity and the spirit of martyrdom for the cause of justice and truth which I have met with in the Western countries have been a great lesson and inspiration to me. I have no doubt in my mind that the West owes its true greatness, not so much to its marvellous training of intellect, as to its spirit of service devoted to the welfare of man. Therefore I speak with a personal feeling of pain and sadness about the collective power which is guiding the helm of Western civilisation. It is a passion, not an ideal. The more success it has brought to Europe, the more costly it will prove to her at last, when the accounts have to be rendered. And the signs are unmistakable, that the accounts have been called for. The time has come when Europe must know that the forcible parasitism which she has been practising upon the two large Continents of the world—the two most unwieldy whales of humanity—must be causing to her moral nature a gradual atrophy and degeneration.

As an example, let me quote the following extract from the concluding chapter of *From the Cape to Cairo,* by Messrs. Grogan and Sharp, two writers who have the power to inculcate their doctrines by precept and example. In their reference to the African they are candid, as when they say, "We have stolen his land. Now we must steal his limbs." These two sentences, carefully articulated, with a smack of enjoyment, have been more clearly explained in the following statement, where some sense of that decency which is the attenuated ghost of a buried conscience, prompts the writers to use the phrase "compulsory labour" in place of the honest word "slavery"; just as the modern politician adroitly avoids the word "injunction" and uses the word "mandate." "Compulsory labour in some form," they say, "is the corollary of our occupation of the country." And they add: "It is pathetic, but it is history," implying thereby that moral sentiments have no serious effect in the history of human beings.

Elsewhere they write: "Either we must give up the country commercially, or we must make the African work. And mere abuse of those who point out the impasse cannot change the facts. We must decide, and soon. Or rather the white man of South Africa will decide." The authors also confess that they have seen too much of the world "to have any lingering belief that Western civilisation benefits native races."

The logic is simple—the logic of egoism. But the argument is simplified by lopping off the greater part of the premise. For these writers seem to hold that the only important question for the white men of South Africa is, how indefinitely to grow fat on ostrich feathers and diamond mines, and dance jazz dances over the misery and degradation of a whole race of fellow-beings of a different colour from their own. Possibly they believe that moral laws have a special domesticated breed of comfortable concessions for the service of the people in power. Possibly they ignore the fact that commercial and political cannibalism, profitably practised upon foreign races, creeps back nearer home; that the cultivation of unwholesome appetites has its final reckoning with the stomach which has been made to serve it. For, after all, man is a spiritual being, and not a mere living money-bag jumping from profit to profit, and breaking the backbone of human races in its financial leapfrog.

Such, however, has been the condition of things for more than a century; and to-day, trying to read the future by the light of the European conflagration, we are asking ourselves everywhere in the East: "Is this frightfully overgrown power really great? It can bruise us from without, but can it add to our wealth of spirit? It can sign peace treaties, but can it give peace?"

It was about two thousand years ago that all-powerful Rome in one of its eastern provinces executed on a cross a simple teacher of an obscure tribe of fishermen. On that day the Roman governor felt no falling off of his appetite or sleep. On that day there was, on the one hand, the agony, the humiliation, the death; on the other, the pomp of pride and festivity in the Governor's palace.

And to-day? To whom, then, shall we bow the head?

> Kasmai devaya havisha vidhema?
>
> (To which God shall we offer oblation?)

We know of an instance in our own history of India, when a great personality, both in his life and voice, struck the keynote of the solemn music of the soul—love for all creatures. And that music crossed seas, mountains, and deserts. Races belonging to different climates, habits, and languages were drawn together, not in the clash of arms, not in the conflict of exploitation, but in harmony of life, in amity and peace. That was creation.

When we think of it, we see at once what the confusion of thought was to which the Western poet, dwelling upon the difference between East and West, referred when he said, "Never the twain shall meet." It is true that they are not yet showing any real sign of meeting. But the reason is because the West has not sent out its humanity to meet the man in the East, but only its machine. Therefore the poet's line has to be changed into something like this:

> Man is man, machine is machine,
> And never the twain shall wed.

You must know that red tape can never be a common human bond; that official sealing-wax can never provide means of mutual attachment; that it is a painful ordeal for human beings to have to receive favours from animated pigeon-holes, and condescensions from printed circulars that give notice but never speak. The presence of the Western people in the East is a human fact. If we are to gain anything from them, it must not be a mere sum-total of legal codes and systems of civil and military services. Man is a great deal more to man than that. We have our human birthright to claim direct help from the man of the West, if he has anything great to give us. It must come to us, not through mere facts in a juxtaposition, but through the spontaneous sacrifice made by those who have the gift, and therefore the responsibility.

Earnestly I ask the poet of the Western world to realise and sing to you with all the great power of music which he has, that the East and the West are ever in search of each other, and that they must meet not merely in the fulness of physical strength, but in fulness of truth; that the right hand, which wields the sword, has the need of the left, which holds the shield of safety.

The East has its seat in the vast plains watched over by the snow-peaked mountains and fertilised by rivers carrying mighty volumes of water to the sea. There, under the blaze of a tropical sun, the physical life has bedimmed the light of its vigour and lessened its claims. There man has had the repose of mind which has ever tried to set itself in harmony with the inner notes of existence. In the silence of sunrise and sunset, and on star-crowded nights, he has sat face to face with the Infinite, waiting for the revelation that opens up the heart of all that there is. He has said, in a rapture of realisation:

"Hearken to me, ye children of the Immortal, who dwell in the Kingdom of Heaven.

I have known, from beyond darkness, the Supreme Person, shining with the radiance of the sun."

The man from the East, with his faith in the eternal, who in his soul had met the touch of the Supreme Person—did he never come to you in the West and speak to you of the Kingdom of Heaven? Did he not unite the East and the West in truth, in the unity of one spiritual bond between all children of the Immortal, in the realisation of one great Personality in all human persons?

Yes, the East did once meet the West profoundly in the growth of her life. Such union became possible, because the East came to the West with the ideal that is creative, and not with the passion that destroys moral bonds. The mystic consciousness of the Infinite, which she brought with her, was greatly needed by the man of the West to give him his balance.

On the other hand, the East must find her own balance in Science—the magnificent gift that the West can bring to her. Truth has its nest as well as its sky. That nest is definite in structure, accurate in law of construction; and though it has to be changed and rebuilt over and over again, the need of it is never-ending and its laws are eternal. For some centuries the East has neglected the nest-building of truth. She has not been attentive to learn its secret. Trying to cross the trackless infinite, the East has relied solely upon her wings. She has spurned the earth, till, buffeted by storms, her wings are hurt and she is tired, sorely needing help. But has she then to be told that the messenger of the sky and the builder of the nest shall never meet?

THE MODERN AGE

THE MODERN AGE

I

WHEREVER man meets man in a living relationship, the meeting finds its natural expression in works of art, the signatures of beauty, in which the mingling of the personal touch leaves its memorial.

On the other hand, a relationship of pure utility humiliates man—it ignores the rights and needs of his deeper nature; it feels no compunction in maltreating and killing things of beauty that can never be restored.

Some years ago, when I set out from Calcutta on my voyage to Japan, the first thing that shocked me, with a sense of personal injury, was the ruthless intrusion of the factories for making gunny-bags on both banks of the Ganges. The blow it gave to me was owing to the precious memory of the days of my boyhood, when the scenery of this river was the only great thing near my birthplace reminding me of the existence of a world which had its direct communication with our innermost spirit.

Calcutta is an upstart town with no depth of sentiment in her face and in her manners. It may truly be said about her genesis:—In the beginning there was the spirit of the Shop, which uttered through its megaphone, "Let there be the Office!" and there was Calcutta. She brought with her no dower of distinction, no majesty of noble or romantic origin; she never gathered around her any great historical associations, any annals of brave sufferings, or memory of mighty deeds. The only thing which gave her the sacred baptism of beauty was the river. I was fortunate enough to be born before the smoke-belching iron dragon had devoured the greater part of the life of its banks; when the landing-stairs descending into its waters, caressed by its tides, appeared to me like the loving arms of the villages clinging to it; when Calcutta, with her up-tilted nose and stony stare, had not completely disowned her foster-mother, rural Bengal, and had not surrendered body and soul to her wealthy paramour, the spirit of the ledger, bound in dead leather.

But as an instance of the contrast of the

different ideal of a different age, incarnated in the form of a town, the memory of my last visit to Benares comes to my mind. What impressed me most deeply, while I was there, was the mother-call of the river Ganges, ever filling the atmosphere with an "unheard melody," attracting the whole population to its bosom every hour of the day. I am proud of the fact that India has felt a most profound love for this river, which nourishes civilisation on its banks, guiding its course from the silence of the hills to the sea with its myriad voices of solitude. The love of this river, which has become one with the love of the best in man, has given rise to this town as an expression of reverence. This is to show that there are sentiments in us which are creative, which do not clamour for gain, but overflow in gifts, in spontaneous generosity of self-sacrifice.

But our minds will nevermore cease to be haunted by the perturbed spirit of the question, "What about gunny-bags?" I admit they are indispensable, and am willing to allow them a place in society, if my opponent will only admit that even gunny-bags should have their limits, and will acknowledge the importance of leisure to man, with space for joy and worship, and a home of wholesale privacy, with associations of chaste love and mutual service. If this concession to humanity be denied or curtailed, and if profit and production are allowed to run amuck, they will play havoc with our love of beauty, of truth, of justice, and also with our love for our fellow-beings. So it comes about that the peasant cultivators of jute, who live on the brink of everlasting famine, are combined against, and driven to lower the price of their labours to the point of blank despair, by those who earn more than cent per cent profit and wallow in the infamy of their wealth. The facts that man is brave and kind, that he is social and generous and self-sacrificing, have some aspect of the complete in them ; but the fact that he is a manufacturer of gunny-bags is too ridiculously small to claim the right of reducing his higher nature to insignificance. The fragmentariness of utility should never forget its subordinate position in human affairs. It must not be permitted to occupy more than its legitimate place and power in society, nor to have the liberty to desecrate the poetry of life, to deaden our sensitiveness to ideals, bragging of its own coarseness as a sign of virility. The pity is that when in the centre of our activities we acknowledge, by some proud name, the supremacy of wanton destructiveness, or production not less wanton, we shut out all the lights of our souls, and in that darkness our conscience and our consciousness of shame are hidden, and our love of freedom is killed.

I do not for a moment mean to imply that in any particular period of history men were free from the disturbance of their lower passions. Selfishness ever had its share in government and trade. Yet there was a struggle to maintain a balance of forces in society; and our passions cherished no delusions about their own rank and value. They contrived no clever devices to hoodwink our moral nature. For in those days our intellect was not tempted to put its weight into the balance on the side of over-greed.

But in recent centuries a devastating change has come over our mentality with regard to the acquisition of money. Whereas in former ages men treated it with condescension, even with disrespect, now they bend their knees to it. That it should be allowed a sufficiently large place in society, there can be no question; but it becomes an outrage when it occupies those seats which are specially reserved for the immortals, by bribing us, tampering with our moral pride, recruiting the best strength of society in a traitor's campaign against human ideals, thus disguising, with the help of pomp and pageantry, its true insignificance. Such a state of things has come to pass because, with the help of science, the possibilities of profit have suddenly become immoderate. The whole of the human world, throughout its length and breadth, has felt the gravitational pull of a giant planet of greed, with concentric rings of innumerable satellites, causing in our society a marked deviation from the moral orbit. In former times the intellectual and spiritual powers of this earth upheld their dignity of independence and were not giddily rocked on the tides of the money market. But, as in the last fatal stages of disease, this fatal influence of money has got into our brain and affected our heart. Like a usurper, it has occupied the throne of high social ideals, using every means, by menace and threat, to seize upon the right, and, tempted by opportunity, presuming to judge it. It has not only science for its ally, but other forces also that have some semblance of religion, such as nation-worship and the idealising of organised selfishness. Its methods are far-reaching and sure. Like the claws of a tiger's paw, they are softly sheathed. Its massacres are invisible, because they are fundamental, attacking the very roots of life. Its plunder is ruthless behind a scientific system of screens, which have the formal appearance of being open and responsible to inquiries. By whitewashing its stains it keeps its respectability unblemished. It makes a liberal use of falsehood in diplomacy, only feeling embarrassed when its evidence is disclosed by others of the trade. An unscrupulous system of propaganda paves the way for widespread misrepresentation. It works up the crowd psychology through regulated hypnotic doses at repeated intervals, administered in bottles with moral labels upon them of soothing colours. In fact, man has been able to make his pursuit of power easier to-day by his art of mitigating the obstructive forces that come from the higher region of his humanity. With his cult of power and his idolatry of money he has, in a great measure, reverted to his primitive barbarism, a barbarism whose path is lit up by the lurid light of intellect. For barbarism is the simplicity of a superficial life. It may be bewildering in its surface adornments and complexities, but it lacks the ideal to impart to it the depth of moral responsibility.

II

Society suffers from a profound feeling of unhappiness, not so much when it is in material poverty as when its members are deprived of a large part of their humanity. This unhappiness goes on smouldering in the subconscious mind of the community till its life is reduced to ashes or a sudden combustion is produced. The repressed personality of man generates an inflammable moral gas deadly in its explosive force.

We have seen in the late war, and also in some of the still more recent events of history, how human individuals freed from moral and spiritual bonds find a boisterous joy in a debauchery of destruction. There is generated a disinterested passion of ravage. Through such catastrophe we can realise what formidable forces of annihilation are kept in check in our communities by bonds of social ideas; nay, made into multitudinous manifestations of beauty and fruitfulness. Thus we know that evils are, like meteors, stray fragments of life, which need the attraction of some great ideal in order to be assimilated with the wholesomeness of creation.

The evil forces are literally outlaws; they only need the control and cadence of spiritual laws to change them into good. The true goodness is not the negation of badness, it is in the mastery of it. Goodness is the miracle which turns the tumult of chaos into a dance of beauty.

In modern society the ideal of wholeness has lost its force. Therefore its different sections have become detached and resolved into their elemental character of forces. Labour is a force; so also is Capital; so are the Government and the People; so are Man and Woman. It is said that when the forces lying latent in even a handful of dust are liberated from their bond of unity, they can lift the buildings of a whole neighbourhood to the height of a mountain. Such disfranchised forces, irresponsible freebooters, may be useful to us for certain purposes, but human habitations standing secure on their foundations are better for us. To own the secret of utilising these forces is a proud fact for us, but the power of self-control and the self-dedication of love are truer subjects for the exultation of mankind. The genii of the Arabian Nights may have in their magic their lure and fascination for us. But the consciousness of God is of another order, infinitely more precious in imparting to our minds ideas of the spiritual power of creation. Yet these genii are abroad everywhere; and even now, after the late war, their devotees are getting ready to play further tricks upon humanity by suddenly spiriting it away to some hill-top of desolation.

III

We know that when, at first, any large body of people in their history became aware of their unity, they expressed it in some popular symbol of divinity. For they felt that their combination was not an arithmetical one; its truth was deeper than the truth of number. They felt that their community was not a mere agglutination but a creation, having upon it the living touch of the infinite Person. The realisation of this truth having been an end in itself, a fulfilment, it gave meaning to self-sacrifice, to the acceptance even of death.

But our modern education is producing a habit of mind which is ever weakening in us the spiritual apprehension of truth—the truth of a person as the ultimate reality of existence. Science has its proper sphere in analysing this world as a construction, just as grammar has its legitimate office in analysing the syntax of a poem. But the world, as a creation, is not a mere construction; it too is more than a syntax. It is a poem, which we are apt to forget when grammar takes exclusive hold of our minds.

Upon the loss of this sense of a universal personality, which is religion, the reign of the machine and of method has been firmly established, and man, humanly speaking, has been made a homeless tramp. As nomads, ravenous and restless, the men from the West have come to us. They have exploited our Eastern humanity for sheer gain of power. This modern meeting of men has not yet received the blessing of God. For it has kept us apart, though railway lines are laid far and wide, and ships are plying from shore to shore to bring us together.

It has been said in the Upanishads:

> Yastu sarvâni bhutâni âtmânyevânupashyati
> Sarva bhuteshu châtmânam na tato vijugupsate.

(He who sees all things in *âtmâ,* in the infinite spirit, and the infinite spirit in all beings, remains no longer unrevealed.)

In the modern civilisation, for which an enormous number of men are used as materials, and human relationships have in a large measure become utilitarian, man is imperfectly revealed.

For man's revelation does not lie in the fact that he is a power, but that he is a spirit. The prevalence of the theory which realises the power of the machine in the universe, and organises men into machines, is like the eruption of Etna, tremendous in its force, in its outburst of fire and fume; but its creeping lava covers up human shelters made by the ages, and its ashes smother life.

IV

The terribly efficient method of repressing personality in the individuals and the races who have failed to resist it has, in the present scientific age, spread all over the world; and in consequence there have appeared signs of a universal disruption which seems not far off. Faced with the possibility of such a disaster, which is sure to affect the successful peoples of the world in their intemperate prosperity, the great Powers of the West are seeking peace, not by curbing their greed, or by giving up the exclusive advantages which they have unjustly acquired, but by concentrating their forces for mutual security.

But can powers find their equilibrium in themselves? Power has to be made secure not only against power, but also against weakness; for there lies the peril of its losing balance. The weak are as great a danger for the strong as quicksands for an elephant. They do not assist progress because they do not resist; they only drag down. The people who grow accustomed to wield absolute power over others are apt to forget that by so doing they generate an unseen force which some day rends that power into pieces. The dumb fury of the downtrodden finds its awful support from the universal law of moral balance. The air which is so thin and unsubstantial gives birth to storms that nothing can resist. This has been proved in history over and over again, and stormy forces arising from the revolt of insulted humanity are openly gathering in the air at the present time.

Yet in the psychology of the strong the lesson is despised and no count taken of the terribleness of the weak. This is the latent ignorance that, like an unsuspected worm, burrows under the bulk of the prosperous. Have we never read of the castle of power, securely buttressed on all sides, in a moment dissolving in air at the explosion caused by the weak and outraged besiegers? Politicians calculate upon the number of mailed hands that are kept on the sword-hilts: they do not possess the third eye to see the great invisible hand that clasps in silence the hand of the helpless and waits its time. The strong form their league by a combination of powers, driving the weak to form their own league alone with their God. I know I am crying in the wilderness when I raise the voice of warning; and while the West is busy with its organisation of a machine-made peace, it will still continue to nourish by its iniquities the underground forces of earthquake in the Eastern Continent. The West seems unconscious that Science, by providing it with more and more power, is tempting it to suicide and encouraging it to accept the challenge of the disarmed; it does not know that the challenge comes from a higher source.

Two prophecies about the world's salvation are cherished in the hearts of the two great religions of the world. They represent the highest expectation of man, thereby indicating his faith in a truth which he instinctively considers as ultimate—the truth of love. These prophecies have not for their vision the fettering of the world and reducing it to tameness by means of a close-linked power forged in the factory of a political steel trust. One of the religions has for its meditation the image of the Buddha who is to come, Maitreya, the Buddha of love; and he is to bring peace. The other religion waits for the coming of Christ. For Christ preached peace when he preached love, when he preached the oneness of the Father with the brothers who are many. And this was the truth of peace. Christ never held that peace was the best policy. For policy is not truth. The calculation of self-interest can never successfully fight the irrational force of passion—the passion which is perversion of love, and which can only be set right by the truth of love. So long as the powers build a league on the foundation of their desire for safety, secure enjoyment of gains, consolidation of past injustice, and putting off the reparation of wrongs, while their fingers still wriggle for greed and reek of blood, rifts will appear in their union; and in future their conflicts will take greater force and magnitude. It is political and commercial egoism which is the evil harbinger of war. By different combinations it changes its shape and dimensions, but not its nature. This egoism is still held sacred, and made a religion; and such a religion, by a mere change of temple, and by new committees of priests, will never save mankind.

We must know that, as, through science and commerce, the realisation of the unity of the material world gives us power, so the realisation of the great spiritual Unity of Man alone can give us peace.

THE SPIRIT OF FREEDOM

THE SPIRIT OF FREEDOM

(A LETTER FROM NEW YORK TO THE AUTHOR'S OWN COUNTRYMEN)

WHEN freedom is not an inner idea which imparts strength to our activities and breadth to our creations, when it is merely a thing of external circumstance, it is like an open space to one who is blindfolded.

In my recent travels in the West I have felt that out there freedom as an idea has become feeble and ineffectual. Consequently a spirit of repression and coercion is fast spreading in the politics and social relationships of the people.

In the age of monarchy the king lived surrounded by a miasma of intrigue. At court there was an endless whispering of lies and calumny, and much plotting and planning among the conspiring courtiers to manipulate the king as the instrument of their own purposes.

In the present age intrigue plays a wider

part, and affects the whole country. The people are drugged with the hashish of false hopes and urged to deeds of frightfulness by the goadings of manufactured panics; their higher feelings are exploited by devious channels of unctuous hypocrisy, their pockets picked under anæsthetics of flattery, their very psychology affected by a conspiracy of money and unscrupulous diplomacy.

In the old order the king was given to understand that he was the freest individual in the world. A greater semblance of external freedom, no doubt, he had than other individuals. But they built for him a gorgeous prison of unreality.

The same thing is happening now with the people of the West. They are flattered into believing that they are free, and they have the sovereign power in their hands. But this power is robbed by hosts of self-seekers, and the horse is captured and stabled because of his gift of freedom over space. The mob-mind is allowed the enjoyment of an apparent liberty, while its true freedom is curtailed on every side. Its thoughts are fashioned according to the plans of organised interest; in its choosing of ideas and forming of opinions it is hindered either by some punitive force or by the constant insinuation of untruths; it is made to dwell in an artificial world of hypnotic phrases. In fact, the people have become the storehouse of a power that attracts round it a swarm of adventurers who are secretly investing its walls to exploit it for their own devices.

Thus it has become more and more evident to me that the ideal of freedom has grown tenuous in the atmosphere of the West. The mentality is that of a slave-owning community, with a mutilated multitude of men tied to its commercial and political treadmill. It is the mentality of mutual distrust and fear. The appalling scenes of inhumanity and injustice, which are growing familiar to us, are the outcome of a psychology that deals with terror. No cruelty can be uglier in its ferocity than the cruelty of the coward. The people who have sacrificed their souls to the passion of profit-making and the drunkenness of power are constantly pursued by phantoms of panic and suspicion, and therefore they are ruthless even where they are least afraid of mischances. They become morally incapable of allowing freedom to others, and in their eagerness to curry favour with the powerful they not only connive at the injustice done by their own partners in political gambling, but participate in it. A perpetual anxiety for the protection of their gains at any cost strikes at the love of freedom and justice, until at length they are ready to forgo liberty for themselves and for others.

My experience in the West, where I have realised the immense power of money and of organised propaganda, — working everywhere behind screens of camouflage, creating an atmosphere of distrust, timidity, and antipathy,—has impressed me deeply with the truth that real freedom is of the mind and spirit ; it can never come to us from outside. He only has freedom who ideally loves freedom himself and is glad to extend it to others. He who cares to have slaves must chain himself to them ; he who builds walls to create exclusion for others builds walls across his own freedom ; he who distrusts freedom in others loses his moral right to it. Sooner or later he is lured into the meshes of physical and moral servility.

Therefore I would urge my own countrymen to ask themselves if the freedom to which they aspire is one of external conditions. Is it merely a transferable commodity ? Have they acquired a true love of freedom ? Have they faith in it ? Are they ready to make space in their society for the minds of their children to grow up in the ideal of human dignity, unhindered by restrictions that are unjust and irrational?

Have we not made elaborately permanent the walls of our social compartments? We are tenaciously proud of their exclusiveness. We boast that, in this world, no other society but our own has come to finality in the classifying of its living members. Yet in our political agitations we conveniently forget that any unnaturalness in the relationship of governors and governed which humiliates us, becomes an outrage when it is artificially fixed under the threat of military persecution.

When India gave voice to immortal thoughts, in the time of fullest vigour of vitality, her children had the fearless spirit of the seekers of truth. The great epic of the soul of our people—the *Mahâbhârata*—gives us a wonderful vision of an overflowing life, full of the freedom of inquiry and experiment. When the age of the Buddha came, humanity was stirred in our country to its uttermost depth. The freedom of mind which it produced expressed itself in a wealth of creation, spreading everywhere in its richness over the continent of Asia. But with the ebb of life in India the spirit of creation died away. It hardened into an age of inert construction. The organic unity of a varied and elastic society gave way to a conventional order which proved its artificial character by its inexorable law of exclusion.

Life has its inequalities, I admit, but they are natural and are in harmony with our vital functions. The head keeps its place apart from the feet, not through some external arrangement or any conspiracy of coercion. If the body is compelled to turn somersaults for an indefinite period, the head never exchanges its relative function for that of the feet. But have our social divisions the same inevitableness of organic law? If we have the hardihood to say "yes" to that question, then how can we blame an alien people for subjecting us to a political order which they are tempted to believe eternal?

By squeezing human beings in the grip of an inelastic system and forcibly holding them fixed, we have ignored the laws of life and growth. We have forced living souls into a permanent passivity, making them incapable of moulding circumstance to their own intrinsic design, and of mastering their own destiny. Borrowing our ideal of life from a dark period of our degeneracy, we have covered up our sensitiveness of soul under the immovable weight of a remote past. We have set up an elaborate ceremonial of cage-worship, and plucked all the feathers from the wings of the living spirit of our people. And for us,—with our centuries of degradation and insult, with the amorphousness of our national unity, with our helplessness before the attack of disasters from without and our unreasoning self-obstructions from within,—the punishment has been terrible. Our stupefaction has become so absolute that we do not even realise that this persistent misfortune, dogging our steps for ages, cannot be a mere accident of history, removable only by another accident from outside.

Unless we have true faith in freedom, knowing it to be creative, manfully taking all its risks, not only do we lose the right to claim freedom in politics, but we also lack the power to maintain it with all our strength. For that would be like assigning the service of God to a confirmed atheist. And men, who contemptuously treat their own brothers and sisters as eternal babies, never to be trusted in the most trivial details of their personal life,—coercing them at every step by the cruel threat of persecution into following a blind lane leading to nowhere, driving a number of them into hypocrisy and into moral inertia,—will fail over and over again to rise to the height of their true and severe responsibility. They will be incapable of holding a just freedom in politics, and of fighting in freedom's cause.

The civilisation of the West has in it the spirit of the machine which must move; and to that blind movement human lives are offered as fuel, keeping up the steam-power. It represents the active aspect of inertia which has the appearance of freedom, but not its truth, and therefore gives rise to slavery both within its boundaries and outside. The present civilisation of India has the constraining power of the mould. It squeezes living man in the grip of rigid regulations, and its repression of individual freedom makes it only too easy for men to be forced into submission of all kinds and degrees. In both of these traditions life is offered up to something which is not life; it is a sacrifice, which has no God for its worship, and is therefore utterly in vain. The West is continually producing mechanical power in excess of its spiritual control, and India has produced a system of mechanical control in excess of its vitality.

THE NATION

THE NATION

THE peoples are living beings. They have their distinct personalities. But nations are organisations of power, and therefore their inner aspects and outward expressions are everywhere monotonously the same. Their differences are merely differences in degree of efficiency.

In the modern world the fight is going on between the living spirit of the people and the methods of nation-organising. It is like the struggle that began in Central Asia between cultivated areas of man's habitation and the continually encroaching desert sands, till the human region of life and beauty was choked out of existence. When the spread of higher ideals of humanity is not held to be important, the hardening method of national efficiency gains a certain strength; and for some limited period of time, at least, it proudly asserts itself as the fittest to survive. But it is the survival of that part of man which is the least living. And this is the reason why dead monotony is the sign of the spread of the Nation. The modern towns, which present the physiognomy due to this dominance of the Nation, are everywhere the same, from San Francisco to London, from London to Tokyo. They show no faces, but merely masks.

The peoples, being living personalities, must have their self-expression, and this leads to their distinctive creations. These creations are literature, art, social symbols and ceremonials. They are like different dishes at one common feast. They add richness to our enjoyment and understanding of truth. They are making the world of man fertile of life and variedly beautiful.

But the nations do not create, they merely produce and destroy. Organisations for production are necessary. Even organisations for destruction may be so. But when, actuated by greed and hatred, they crowd away into a corner the living man who creates, then the harmony is lost, and the people's history runs at a break-neck speed towards some fatal catastrophe.

Humanity, where it is living, is guided by

inner ideals; but where it is a dead organisation it becomes impervious to them. Its building process is only an external process, and in its response to the moral guidance it has to pass through obstacles that are gross and non-plastic.

Man as a person has his individuality, which is the field where his spirit has its freedom to express itself and to grow. The professional man carries a rigid crust around him which has very little variation and hardly any elasticity. This professionalism is the region where men specialise their knowledge and organise their power, mercilessly elbowing each other in their struggle to come to the front. Professionalism is necessary, without doubt; but it must not be allowed to exceed its healthy limits, to assume complete mastery over the personal man, making him narrow and hard, exclusively intent upon pursuit of success at the cost of his faith in ideals.

In ancient India professions were kept within limits by social regulation. They were considered primarily as social necessities, and in the second place as the means of livelihood for individuals. Thus man, being free from the constant urging of unbounded competition, could have leisure to cultivate his nature in its completeness.

The Cult of the Nation is the professionalism of the people. This cult is becoming their greatest danger, because it is bringing them enormous success, making them impatient of the claims of higher ideals. The greater the amount of success, the stronger are the conflicts of interest and jealousy and hatred which are aroused in men's minds, thereby making it more and more necessary for other peoples, who are still living, to stiffen into nations. With the growth of nationalism, man has become the greatest menace to man. Therefore the continual presence of panic goads that very nationalism into ever-increasing menace.

Crowd psychology is a blind force. Like steam and other physical forces, it can be utilised for creating a tremendous amount of power. And therefore rulers of men, who, out of greed and fear, are bent upon turning their peoples into machines of power, try to train this crowd psychology for their special purposes. They hold it to be their duty to foster in the popular mind universal panic, unreasoning pride in their own race, and hatred of others. Newspapers, school-books, and even religious services are made use of for this object; and those who have the courage to express their disapprobation of this blind and impious cult are either punished in the law-courts, or are socially ostracised. The individual thinks, even when he feels; but the same individual, when he feels with the crowd, does not reason at all. His moral sense becomes blurred. This suppression of higher humanity in crowd minds is productive of enormous strength. For the crowd mind is essentially primitive; its forces are elemental. Therefore the Nation is for ever watching to take advantage of this enormous power of darkness.

The people's instinct of self-preservation has been made dominant at particular times of crisis. Then, for the time being, the consciousness of its solidarity becomes aggressively wide-awake. But in the Nation this hyper-consciousness is kept alive for all time by artificial means. A man has to act the part of a policeman when he finds his house invaded by burglars. But if that remains his normal condition, then his consciousness of his household becomes acute and over-wrought, making him fly at every stranger passing near his house. This intensity of self-consciousness is nothing of which a man should feel proud; certainly it is not healthful. In like manner, incessant self-consciousness in a nation is highly injurious for the people. It serves its immediate purpose, but at the cost of the eternal in man.

When a whole body of men train themselves for a particular narrow purpose, it becomes a common interest with them to keep up that purpose and preach absolute loyalty to it. Nationalism is the training of a whole people for a narrow ideal; and when it gets hold of their minds it is sure to lead them to moral degeneracy and intellectual blindness. We cannot but hold firm the faith that this Age of Nationalism, of gigantic vanity and selfishness, is only a passing phase in civilisation, and those who are making permanent arrangements for accommodating this temporary mood of history will be unable to fit themselves for the coming age, when the true spirit of freedom will have sway.

With the unchecked growth of Nationalism the moral foundation of man's civilisation is unconsciously undergoing a change. The ideal of the social man is unselfishness, but the ideal of the Nation, like that of the professional man, is selfishness. This is why selfishness in the individual is condemned, while in the nation it is extolled, which leads to hopeless moral blindness, confusing the religion of the people with the religion of the nation. Therefore, to take an example, we find men more and more convinced of the superior claims of Christianity, merely because Christian nations are in possession of the greater part of the world. It is like supporting a robber's religion by quoting the amount of his stolen property. Nations celebrate their successful massacre of men in their churches. They forget that Thugs also ascribed their success in manslaughter to the favour of their goddess. But in the case of the latter their goddess frankly represented the principle of destruction. It was the criminal tribe's own murderous instinct deified—the instinct, not of one individual, but of the whole community, and therefore held sacred. In the same manner, in modern churches, selfishness, hatred and vanity in their collective aspect of national instincts do not scruple to share the homage paid to God.

Of course, pursuit of self-interest need not be wholly selfish; it can even be in harmony with the interest of all. Therefore, ideally speaking, the nationalism, which stands for the expression of the collective self-interest of a people, need not be ashamed of itself if it maintains its true limitations. But what we see in practice is, that every nation which has prospered has done so through its career of aggressive selfishness either in commercial adventures or in foreign possessions, or in both. And this material prosperity not only feeds continually the selfish instincts of the people, but impresses men's minds with the lesson that, for a nation, selfishness is a necessity and therefore a virtue. It is the emphasis laid in Europe upon the idea of the Nation's constant increase of power, which is becoming the greatest danger to man, both in its direct activity and its power of infection.

We must admit that evils there are in human nature, in spite of our faith in moral laws and our training in self-control. But they carry on their foreheads their own brand of infamy, their very success adding to their monstrosity. All through man's history there will be some who suffer, and others who cause suffering. The conquest of evil will never be a fully accomplished fact, but a continuous process like the process of burning in a flame.

In former ages, when some particular people became turbulent and tried to rob others of their human rights, they sometimes achieved success and sometimes failed. And it amounted to nothing more than that. But when this idea of the Nation, which has met with universal acceptance in the present day, tries to pass off the cult of collective selfishness as a moral duty, simply because that selfishness is gigantic in stature, it not only commits depredation, but attacks the very vitals of humanity. It unconsciously generates in people's minds an attitude of defiance against moral law. For men are taught by repeated devices the lesson that the Nation is greater than the people, while yet it scatters to the winds the moral law that the people have held sacred.

It has been said that a disease becomes most acutely critical when the brain is affected. For it is the brain that is constantly directing the siege against all disease forces. The spirit of national selfishness is that brain disease of a people which shows itself in red eyes and clenched fists, in violence of talk and movements, all the while shattering its natural restorative powers. But the power of self-sacrifice, together with the moral faculty of sympathy and co-operation, is the guiding spirit of social vitality. Its function is to maintain a beneficent relation of harmony with its surroundings. But when it begins to ignore the moral law which is universal and uses it only within the bounds of its own narrow sphere, then its strength becomes like the strength of madness which ends in self-destruction.

What is worse, this aberration of a people, decked with the showy title of "patriotism," proudly walks abroad, passing itself off as a highly moral influence. Thus it has spread its inflammatory contagion all over the world, proclaiming its fever flush to be the best sign of health. It is causing in the hearts of peoples, naturally inoffensive, a feeling of envy at not having their temperature as high as that of their delirious neighbours and not being able to cause as much mischief, but merely having to suffer from it.

I have often been asked by my Western friends how to cope with this evil, which has attained such sinister strength and vast dimensions. In fact, I have often been blamed for merely giving warning, and offering no alternative. When we suffer as a result of a particular system, we believe that some other system would bring us better luck. We are apt to forget that all systems produce evil sooner or later, when the psychology which is at the root of them is wrong. The system which is national to-day may assume the shape of the international to-morrow; but so long as men have not forsaken their idolatry of primitive instincts and collective passions, the new system will only become a new instrument of suffering. And because we are trained to confound efficient system with moral goodness itself, every ruined system makes us more and more distrustful of moral law.

Therefore I do not put my faith in any new institution, but in the individuals all over the world who think clearly, feel nobly, and act rightly, thus becoming the channels of moral truth. Our moral ideals do not work with chisels and hammers. Like trees, they spread their roots in the soil and their branches in the sky, without consulting any architect for their plans.

WOMAN AND HOME

WOMAN AND HOME

CREATIVE expressions attain their perfect form through emotions modulated. Woman has that expression natural to her—a cadence of restraint in her behaviour, producing poetry of life. She has been an inspiration to man, guiding, most often unconsciously, his restless energy into an immense variety of creations in literature, art, music and religion. This is why, in India, woman has been described as the symbol of Shakti, the creative power.

But if woman begins to believe that, though biologically her function is different from that of man, psychologically she is identical with him; if the human world in its mentality becomes exclusively male, then before long it will be reduced to utter inanity. For life finds its truth and beauty, not in any exaggeration of sameness, but in harmony.

If woman's nature were identical with man's,

if Eve were a mere tautology of Adam, it would only give rise to a monotonous superfluity. But that she was not so was proved by the banishment she secured from a ready-made Paradise. She had the instinctive wisdom to realise that it was her mission to help her mate in creating a Paradise of their own on earth, whose ideal she was to supply with her life, whose materials were to be produced and gathered by her comrade.

However, it is evident that an increasing number of women in the West are ready to assert that their difference from men is unimportant. The reason for the vehement utterance of such a paradox cannot be ignored. It is a rebellion against a necessity, which is not equal for both the partners.

Love in all forms has its obligations, and the love that binds women to their children binds them to their homes. But necessity is a tyrant, making us submit to injury and indignity, allowing advantage over us to those who are wholly or comparatively free from its burden. Such has been the case in the social relationship between man and woman. Along with the difference inherent in their respective natures, there have grown up between them inequalities fostered by circumstances. Man is not handicapped by the same biological and psychological responsibilities as woman, and therefore he has the liberty to give her the security of home. This liberty exacts payment when it offers its boon, because to give or to withhold the gift is within its power. It is the unequal freedom in their mutual relationships which has made the weight of life's tragedies so painfully heavy for woman to bear.

Some mitigation of her disadvantage has been effected by her rendering herself and her home a luxury to man. She has accentuated those qualities in herself which insidiously impose their bondage over her mate, some by pandering to his weakness, and some by satisfying his higher nature, till the sex-consciousness in our society has grown abnormal and overpowering. There is no actual objection to this in itself, for it offers a stimulus, acting in the depth of life, which leads to creative exuberance. But a great deal of it is a forced growth of compulsion bearing seeds of degradation. In those ages when men acknowledged spiritual perfection to be their object, women were denounced as the chief obstacle in their way. The constant and conscious exercise of allurements, which gave women their power, attacked the weak spots in man's nature, and by doing so added to its weakness. For all relationships tainted with repression of freedom must become sources of degeneracy to the strong who impose such repression.

Balance of power, however, between man and woman was in a measure established when home wielded a strong enough attraction to make men accept its obligations. But at last the time has come when the material ambition of man has assumed such colossal proportions that home is in danger of losing its centre of gravity for him, and he is receding farther and farther from its orbit.

The arid zone in the social life is spreading fast. The simple comforts of home, made precious by the touch of love, are giving way to luxuries that can only have their full extension in the isolation of self-centred life. Hotels are being erected on the ruins of homes; productions are growing more stupendous than creations; and most men have, for the materials of their happiness and recreation, their dogs and horses, their pipes, guns, and gambling clubs.

Reactions and rebellions, not being normal in their character, go on hurting truth until peace is restored. Therefore, when woman refuses to acknowledge the distinction between her life and that of man, she does not convince us of its truth, but only proves to us that she is suffering. All great sufferings indicate some wrong somewhere. In the present case, the wrong is in woman's lack of freedom in her relationship with man, which compels her to turn her disabilities into attractions, and to use untruths as her allies in the battle of life, while she is suffering from the precariousness of her position.

From the beginning of our society, women have naturally accepted the training which imparts to their life and to their home a spirit of harmony. It is their instinct to perform their services in such a manner that these, through beauty, might be raised from the domain of slavery to the realm of grace. Women have tried to prove that in the building up of social life they are artists and not artisans. But all expressions of beauty lose their truth when compelled to accept the patronage of the gross and the indifferent. Therefore when necessity drives women to fashion their lives to the taste of the insensitive or the sensual, then the whole thing becomes a tragedy of desecration. Society is full of such tragedies. Many of the laws and social regulations guiding the relationships of man and woman are relics of a barbaric age, when the brutal pride of an exclusive possession had its dominance in human relations, such as those of parents and children, husbands and wives, masters and servants, teachers and disciples. The vulgarity of it still persists in the social bond between the sexes because of the economic helplessness of woman. Nothing makes us so stupidly mean as the sense of superiority which the power of the purse confers upon us.

The powers of muscle and of money have opportunities of immediate satisfaction, but the power of the ideal must have infinite patience. The man who sells his goods, or fulfils his contract, is cheated if he fails to realise payment, but he who gives form to some ideal may never get his due and be fully paid. What I have felt in the women of India is the consciousness of this ideal—their simple faith in the sanctity of devotion lighted by love which is held to be divine. True womanliness is regarded in our country as the saintliness of love. It is not merely praised there, but literally worshipped; and she who is gifted with it is called *Devi*, as one revealing in herself Woman, the Divine. That this has not been a mere metaphor to us is because, in India, our mind is familiar with the idea of God in an eternal feminine aspect. Thus the Eastern woman, who is deeply aware in her heart of the sacredness of her mission, is a constant education to man. It has to be admitted that there are chances of such an influence failing to penetrate the callousness of the coarse-minded; but that is the destiny of all manifestations whose value is not in success or reward in honour.

Woman has to be ready to suffer. She cannot allow her emotions to be dulled or polluted, for these are to create her life's atmosphere, apart from which her world would be dark and dead. This leaves her heart without any protection of insensibility, at the mercy of the hurts and insults of life. Women of India, like women everywhere, have their share of suffering, but it radiates through the ideal, and becomes, like sunlight, a creative force in their world. Our women know by heart the legends of the great women of the epic age—Savitri who by the power of love conquered death, and Sita who had no other reward for her life of sacrifice but the sacred majesty of sorrow. They know that it is their duty to make this life an image of the life eternal, and that love's mission truly performed has a spiritual meaning. It is a religious responsibility for them to live the life which is their own. For their activity is not for money-making, or organising power, or intellectually probing the mystery of existence, but for establishing and maintaining human relationships requiring the highest moral qualities. It is the consciousness of the spiritual character of their life's work, which lifts them above the utilitarian standard of the immediate and the passing, surrounds them with the dignity of the eternal, and transmutes their suffering and sorrow into a crown of light.

I must guard myself from the risk of a possible misunderstanding. The permanent significance of home is not in the narrowness of its enclosure, but in an eternal moral idea. It represents the truth of human relationship; it reveals loyalty and love for the personality of man. Let us take a wider view, in a perspective truer than can be found in its present conventional associations. With the discovery and development of agriculture there came a period of settled life in our history. The nomad ever moved on with his tents and cattle; he explored space and exploited its contents. The cultivator of land explored time in its immensity, for he had leisure. Comparatively secured from the uncertainty of his outer resources, he had the opportunity to deal with his moral resources in the realm of human truth. This is why agricultural civilisation, like that of India and China, is essentially a civilisation of human relationship, of the adjustment of mutual obligations. It is deep-rooted in the inner life of man. Its basis is co-operation and not competition. In other words, its principle is the principle of home, to which all its outer adventures are subordinated.

In the meanwhile, the nomadic life with its predatory instinct of exploitation has developed into a great civilisation. It is immensely proud and strong, killing leisure and pursuing opportunities. It minimises the claims of personal relationship and is jealously careful of its unhampered freedom for acquiring wealth and asserting its will upon others. Its burden is the burden of things, which grows heavier and more complex every day, disregarding the human and the spiritual. Its powerful pressure from all sides narrows the limits of home, the personal region of the human world. Thus, in this region of life, women are every day hustled out of their shelter for want of accommodation.

But such a state of things can never have the

effect of changing woman into man. On the contrary, it will lead her to find her place in the unlimited range of society, and the Guardian Spirit of the personal in human nature will extend the ministry of woman over all developments of life. Habituated to deal with the world as a machine, man is multiplying his materials, banishing away his happiness and sacrificing love to comfort, which is an illusion. At last the present age has sent its cry to women, asking her to come out from her segregation in order to restore the spiritual supremacy of all that is human in the world of humanity. She has been aroused to remember that womanliness is not chiefly decorative. It is like that vital health, which not only imparts the bloom of beauty to the body, but joy to the mind and perfection to life.

AN EASTERN UNIVERSITY

AN EASTERN UNIVERSITY

In the midst of much that is discouraging in the present state of the world, there is one symptom of vital promise. Asia is awakening. This great event, if it be but directed along the right lines, is full of hope, not only for Asia herself, but for the whole world.

On the other hand, it has to be admitted that the relationship of the West with the East, growing more and more complex and widespread for over two centuries, far from attaining its true fulfilment, has given rise to a universal spirit of conflict. The consequent strain and unrest have profoundly disturbed Asia, and antipathetic forces have been accumulating for years in the depth of the Eastern mind.

The meeting of the East and the West has remained incomplete, because the occasions of it have not been disinterested. The political and commercial adventures carried on by

Western races—very often by force and against the interest and wishes of the countries they have dealt with—have created a moral alienation, which is deeply injurious to both parties. The perils threatened by this unnatural relationship have long been contemptuously ignored by the West. But the blind confidence of the strong in their apparent invincibility has often led them, from their dream of security, into terrible surprises of history.

It is not the fear of danger or loss to one people or another, however, which is most important. The demoralising influence of the constant estrangement between the two hemispheres, which affects the baser passions of man, —pride, greed and hypocrisy on the one hand; fear, suspiciousness and flattery on the other,—has been developing, and threatens us with a world-wide spiritual disaster.

The time has come when we must use all our wisdom to understand the situation, and to control it, with a stronger trust in moral guidance than in any array of physical forces.

In the beginning of man's history his first social object was to form a community, to grow into a people. At that early period, individuals were gathered together within geographical enclosures. But in the present age, with its facility of communication, geographical barriers have almost lost their reality, and the great federation of men, which is waiting either to find its true scope or to break asunder in a final catastrophe, is not a meeting of individuals, but of various human races. Now the problem before us is of one single country, which is this earth, where the races as individuals must find both their freedom of self-expression and their bond of federation. Mankind must realise a unity, wider in range, deeper in sentiment, stronger in power than ever before. Now that the problem is large, we have to solve it on a bigger scale, to realise the God in man by a larger faith and to build the temple of our faith on a sure and world-wide basis.

The first step towards realisation is to create opportunities for revealing the different peoples to one another. This can never be done in those fields where the exploiting utilitarian spirit is supreme. We must find some meeting-ground, where there can be no question of conflicting interests. One of such places is the University, where we can work together in a common pursuit of truth, share together our common heritage, and realise that artists in all parts of the world have created forms of beauty, scientists discovered secrets of the universe, philosophers solved the problems of existence, saints made the truth of the spiritual world organic in their own lives, not merely for some particular race to which they belonged, but for all mankind. When the science of meteorology knows the earth's atmosphere as continuously one, affecting the different parts of the world differently, but in a harmony of adjustments, it knows and attains truth. And so, too, we must know that the great mind of man is one, working through the many differences which are needed to ensure the full result of its fundamental unity. When we understand this truth in a disinterested spirit, it teaches us to respect all the differences in man that are real, yet remain conscious of our oneness; and to know that perfection of unity is not in uniformity, but in harmony.

This is the problem of the present age. The East, for its own sake and for the sake of the world, must not remain unrevealed. The deepest source of all calamities in history is misunderstanding. For where we do not understand, we can never be just.

Being strongly impressed with the need and the responsibility, which every individual to-day must realise according to his power, I have formed the nucleus of an International University in India, as one of the best means of promoting mutual understanding between the East and the West. This Institution, according to the plan I have in mind, will invite students from the West to study the different systems of Indian philosophy, literature, art and music in their proper environment, encouraging them to carry on research work in collaboration with the scholars already engaged in this task.

India has her renaissance. She is preparing to make her contribution to the world of the future. In the past she produced her great culture, and in the present age she has an equally important contribution to make to the culture of the New World which is emerging from the wreckage of the Old. This is a momentous period of her history, pregnant with precious possibilities, when any disinterested offer of co-operation from any part of the West will have an immense moral value, the memory of which will become brighter as the regeneration of the East grows in vigour and creative power.

The Western Universities give their students an opportunity to learn what all the European peoples have contributed to their Western culture. Thus the intellectual mind of the West has been luminously revealed to the world. What is needed to complete this illumination is for the East to collect its own scattered lamps and offer them to the enlightenment of the world.

There was a time when the great countries of Asia had, each of them, to nurture its own civilisation apart in comparative seclusion. Now has come the age of co-ordination and co-operation. The seedlings that were reared within narrow plots must now be transplanted into the open fields. They must pass the test of the world-market, if their maximum value is to be obtained.

But before Asia is in a position to co-operate with the culture of Europe, she must base her own structure on a synthesis of all the different cultures which she has. When, taking her stand on such a culture, she turns toward the West, she will take, with a confident sense of mental freedom, her own view of truth, from her own vantage-ground, and open a new vista of thought to the world. Otherwise, she will allow her priceless inheritance to crumble into dust, and, trying to replace it clumsily with feeble imitations of the West, make herself superfluous, cheap and ludicrous. If she thus loses her individuality and her specific power to exist, will it in the least help the rest of the world? Will not her terrible bankruptcy involve also the Western mind? If the whole world grows at last into an exaggerated West, then such an illimitable parody of the modern age will die, crushed beneath its own absurdity.

In this belief, it is my desire to extend by degrees the scope of this University on simple lines, until it comprehends the whole range of Eastern cultures—the Aryan, Semitic, Mongolian and others. Its object will be to reveal the Eastern mind to the world.

Of one thing I felt certain during my travels in Europe, that a genuine interest has been roused there in the philosophy and the arts of the East, from which the Western mind seeks fresh inspiration of truth and beauty. Once the East had her reputation of fabulous wealth, and the seekers were attracted from across the sea. Since then, the shrine of wealth has changed its site. But the East is famed also for her storage of wisdom, harvested by her patriarchs from long successive ages of spiritual endeavour. And when, as now, in the midst of the pursuit of power and wealth, there rises the cry of privation from the famished spirit of man, an opportunity is offered to the East to offer her store to those who need it.

Once upon a time we were in possession of such a thing as our own mind in India. It was living. It thought, it felt, it expressed itself. It was receptive as well as productive. That this mind could be of any use in the process, or in the end, of our education was overlooked by our modern educational dispensation. We are provided with buildings and books and other magnificent burdens calculated to suppress our mind. The latter was treated like a library-shelf solidly made of wood, to be loaded with leather-bound volumes of second-hand information. In consequence, it has lost its own colour and character, and has borrowed polish from the carpenter's shop. All this has cost us money, and also our finer ideas, while our intellectual vacancy has been crammed with what is described in official reports as Education. In fact, we have bought our spectacles at the expense of our eyesight.

In India our goddess of learning is *Saraswati*. My audience in the West, I am sure, will be glad to know that her complexion is white. But the signal fact is that she is living and she is a woman, and her seat is on a lotus-flower. The symbolic meaning of this is, that she dwells in the centre of life and the heart of all existence, which opens itself in beauty to the light of heaven.

The Western education which we have chanced to know is impersonal. Its complexion is also white, but it is the whiteness of the white-washed class-room walls. It dwells in the cold-storage compartments of lessons and the ice-packed minds of the schoolmasters. The effect which it had on my mind when, as a boy, I was compelled to go to school, I have described elsewhere. My feeling was very much the same as a tree might have, which was not allowed to live its full life, but was cut down to be made into packing-cases.

The introduction of this education was not a part of the solemn marriage ceremony which was to unite the minds of the East and West in mutual understanding. It represented an artificial method of training specially calculated to produce the carriers of the white man's burden. This want of ideals still clings to our education system, though our Universities have latterly burdened their syllabus with a greater number of subjects than before. But it is only like adding to the bags of wheat the bullock carries to market; it does not make the bullock any better off.

Mind, when long deprived of its natural food of truth and freedom of growth, develops an unnatural craving for success; and our students have fallen victims to the mania for success in examinations. Success consists in obtaining the largest number of marks with the strictest economy of knowledge. It is a deliberate cultivation of disloyalty to truth, of intellectual dishonesty, of a foolish imposition by which the mind is encouraged to rob itself. But as we are by means of it made to forget the existence of mind, we are supremely happy at the result. We pass examinations, and shrivel up into clerks, lawyers and police inspectors, and we die young.

Universities should never be made into mechanical organisations for collecting and distributing knowledge. Through them the people should offer their intellectual hospitality, their wealth of mind to others, and earn their proud right in return to receive gifts from the rest of the world. But in the whole length and breadth of India there is not a single University established in the modern time where a foreign or an

Indian student can properly be acquainted with the best products of the Indian mind. For that we have to cross the sea, and knock at the doors of France and Germany. Educational institutions in our country are India's alms-bowl of knowledge; they lower our intellectual self-respect; they encourage us to make a foolish display of decorations composed of borrowed feathers.

This it was that led me to found a school in Bengal, in face of many difficulties and discouragements, and in spite of my own vocation as a poet, who finds his true inspiration only when he forgets that he is a schoolmaster. It is my hope that in this school a nucleus has been formed, round which an indigenous University of our own land will find its natural growth—a University which will help India's mind to concentrate and to be fully conscious of itself; free to seek the truth and make this truth its own wherever found, to judge by its own standard, give expression to its own creative genius, and offer its wisdom to the guests who come from other parts of the world.

Man's intellect has a natural pride in its own aristocracy, which is the pride of its culture. Culture only acknowledges the excellence whose criticism is in its inner perfection, not in any external success. When this pride succumbs to some compulsion of necessity or lure of material advantage, it brings humiliation to the intellectual man. Modern India, through her very education, has been made to suffer this humiliation. Once she herself provided her children with a culture which was the product of her own ages of thought and creation. But it has been thrust aside, and we are made to tread the mill of passing examinations, not for learning anything, but for notifying that we are qualified for employments under organisations conducted in English. Our educated community is not a cultured community, but a community of qualified candidates. Meanwhile the proportion of possible employments to the number of claimants has gradually been growing narrower, and the consequent disaffection has been widespread. At last the very authorities who are responsible for this are blaming their victims. Such is the perversity of human nature. It bears its worst grudge against those it has injured.

It is as if some tribe which had the primitive habit of decorating its tribal members with birds' plumage were some day to hold these very birds guilty of the crime of being extinct. There are belated attempts on the part of our governors to read us pious homilies about disinterested love of learning, while the old machinery goes on working, whose product is not education but certificates. It is good to remind the fettered bird that its wings are for soaring; but it is better to cut the chain which is holding it to its perch. The most pathetic feature of the tragedy is that the bird itself has learnt to use its chain for its ornament, simply because the chain jingles in fairly respectable English.

In the Bengali language there is a modern maxim which can be translated, "He who learns to read and write rides in a carriage and pair." In English there is a similar proverb, "Knowledge is power." It is an offer of a prospective bribe to the student, a promise of an ulterior reward which is more important than knowledge itself. Temptations, held before us as inducements to be good or to pursue uncongenial paths, are most often flimsy lies or half-truths, such as the oft-quoted maxim of respectable piety, "Honesty is the best policy," at which politicians all over the world seem to laugh in their sleeves. But unfortunately, education conducted under a special providence of purposefulness, of eating the fruit of knowledge from the wrong end, *does* lead one to that special paradise on earth, the daily rides in one's own carriage and pair. And the West, I have heard from authentic sources, is aspiring in its education after that special cultivation of worldliness.

Where society is comparatively simple and obstructions are not too numerous, we can clearly see how the life-process guides education in its vital purpose. The system of folk-education, which is indigenous to India, but is dying out, was one with the people's life. It flowed naturally through the social channels and made its way everywhere. It is a system of widespread irrigation of culture. Its teachers, specially trained men, are in constant requisition, and find crowded meetings in our villages, where they repeat the best thoughts and express the ideals of the land in the most effective form. The mode of instruction includes the recitation of epics, expounding of the scriptures, reading from the Puranas, which are the classical records of old history, performance of plays founded upon the early myths and legends, dramatic narration of the lives of ancient heroes, and the singing in chorus of songs from the old religious literature. Evidently, according to this system, the best function of education is to enable us to realise that to live as a man is great, requiring profound philosophy for its ideal, poetry for its expression, and heroism in its conduct. Owing to this vital method of culture the common people of India, though technically illiterate, have been made conscious of the sanctity of social relationships, entailing constant sacrifice and self-control, urged and supported by ideals collectively expressed in one word, *Dharma*.

Such a system of education may sound too simple for the complexities of modern life. But the fundamental principle of social life in its different stages of development remains the same; and in no circumstance can the truth be ignored that all human complexities must harmonise in organic unity with life, failing which there will be endless conflict. Most things in the civilised world occupy more than their legitimate space. Much of their burden is needless. By bearing this burden civilised man may be showing great strength, but he displays little skill. To the gods, viewing this from on high, it must seem like the flounderings of a giant who has got out of his depth and knows not how to swim.

The main source of all forms of voluntary slavery is the desire of gain. It is difficult to fight against this when modern civilisation is tainted with such a universal contamination of avarice. I have realised it myself in the little boys of my own school. For the first few years there is no trouble. But as soon as the upper class is reached, their worldly wisdom—the malady of the aged—begins to assert itself. They rebelliously insist that they must no longer learn, but rather pass examinations. Professions in the modern age are more numerous and lucrative than ever before. They need specialisation of training and knowledge, tempting education to yield its spiritual freedom to the claims of utilitarian ambitions. But man's deeper nature is hurt; his smothered life seeks to be liberated from the suffocating folds and sensual ties of prosperity. And this is why we find almost everywhere in the world a growing dissatisfaction with the prevalent system of teaching, which betrays the encroachment of senility and worldly prudence over pure intellect.

In India, also, a vague feeling of discontent has given rise to numerous attempts at establishing national schools and colleges. But, unfortunately, our very education has been successful in depriving us of our real initiative and our courage of thought. The training we get in our schools has the constant implication in it that it is not for us to produce but to borrow. And we are casting about to borrow our educational plans from European institutions. The trampled plants of Indian corn are dreaming of recouping their harvest from the neighbouring wheat fields. To change the figure, we forget that, for proficiency in walking, it is better to train the muscles of our own legs than to strut upon wooden ones of foreign make, although they clatter and cause more surprise at our skill in using them than if they were living and real.

But when we go to borrow help from a foreign neighbourhood we are apt to overlook the real source of help behind all that is external and apparent. Had the deep-water fishes happened to produce a scientist who chose the jumping of a monkey for his research work, I am sure he would give most of the credit to the branches of the trees and very little to the monkey itself. In a foreign University we see the branching wildernesses of its buildings, furniture, regulations, and syllabus, but the monkey, which is a difficult creature to catch and more difficult to manufacture, we are likely to treat as a mere accident of minor importance. It is convenient for us to overlook the fact that among the Europeans the living spirit of the University is widely spread in their society, their parliament, their literature, and the numerous activities of their corporate life. In all these functions they are in perpetual touch with the great personality of the land which is creative and heroic in its constant acts of self-expression and self-sacrifice. They have their thoughts published in their books as well as through the medium of living men who think those thoughts, and who criticise, compare and disseminate them. Some at least of the drawbacks of their academic education are redeemed by the living energy of the intellectual personality pervading their social organism. It is like the stagnant reservoir of water which finds its purification in the showers of rain to which it keeps itself open. But, to our misfortune, we have in India all the furniture of the European University except the human teacher. We have, instead, mere purveyors of book-lore in whom the paper god of the bookshop has been made vocal.

A most important truth, which we are apt

to forget, is that a teacher can never truly teach unless he is still learning himself. A lamp can never light another lamp unless it continues to burn its own flame. The teacher who has come to the end of his subject, who has no living traffic with his knowledge, but merely repeats his lessons to his students, can only load their minds ; he cannot quicken them. Truth not only must inform but inspire. If the inspiration dies out, and the information only accumulates, then truth loses its infinity. The greater part of our learning in the schools has been wasted because, for most of our teachers, their subjects are like dead specimens of once living things, with which they have a learned acquaintance, but no communication of life and love.

The educational institution, therefore, which I have in mind has primarily for its object the constant pursuit of truth, from which the imparting of truth naturally follows. It must not be a dead cage in which living minds are fed with food artificially prepared. It should be an open house, in which students and teachers are at one. They must live their complete life together, dominated by a common aspiration for truth and a need of sharing all the delights of culture. In former days the great master-craftsmen had students in their workshops where they co-operated in shaping things to perfection. That was the place where knowledge could become living—that knowledge which not only has its substance and law, but its atmosphere subtly informed by a creative personality. For intellectual knowledge also has its aspect of creative art, in which the man who explores truth expresses something which is human in him—his enthusiasm, his courage, his sacrifice, his honesty, and his skill. In merely academical teaching we find subjects, but not the man who pursues the subjects; therefore the vital part of education remains incomplete.

For our Universities we must claim, not labelled packages of truth and authorised agents to distribute them, but truth in its living association with her lovers and seekers and discoverers. Also we must know that the concentration of the mind-forces scattered throughout the country is the most important mission of a University, which, like the nucleus of a living cell, should be the centre of the intellectual life of the people.

The bringing about of an intellectual unity in India is, I am told, difficult to the verge of impossibility owing to the fact that India has so many different languages. Such a statement is as unreasonable as to say that man, because he has a diversity of limbs, should find it impossible to realise life's unity in himself, and that only an earthworm composed of a tail and nothing else could truly know that it had a body.

Let us admit that India is not like any one of the great countries of Europe, which has its own separate language; but is rather like Europe herself, branching out into different peoples with many different languages. And yet Europe has a common civilisation, with an intellectual unity which is not based upon uniformity of language. It is true that in the earlier stages of her culture the whole of Europe had Latin for her learned tongue. That was in her intellectual budding time, when all her petals of self-expression were closed in one point. But the perfection of her mental unfolding was not represented by the singularity of her literary vehicle. When the great European countries found their individual languages, then only the true federation of cultures became possible in the West, and the very differences of the channels made the commerce of ideas in Europe so richly copious and so variedly active. We can well imagine what the loss to European civilisation would be if

France, Italy and Germany, and England herself, had not through their separate agencies contributed to the common coffer their individual earnings.

There was a time with us when India had her common language of culture in Sanskrit. But, for the complete commerce of her thought, she required that all her vernaculars should attain their perfect powers, through which her different peoples might manifest their idiosyncrasies; and this could never be done through a foreign tongue.

In the United States, in Canada and other British Colonies, the language of the people is English. It has a great literature which had its birth and growth in the history of the British Islands. But when this language, with all its products and acquisitions, matured by ages on its own mother soil, is carried into foreign lands, which have their own separate history and their own life-growth, it must constantly hamper the indigenous growth of culture and destroy individuality of judgement and the perfect freedom of self-expression. The inherited wealth of the English language, with all its splendour, becomes an impediment when taken into different surroundings, just as when lungs are given to the whale in the sea. If such is the case even with races whose grandmother-tongue naturally continues to be their own mother-tongue, one can imagine what sterility it means for a people which accepts, for its vehicle of culture, an altogether foreign language. A language is not like an umbrella or an overcoat, that can be borrowed by unconscious or deliberate mistake; it is like the living skin itself. If the body of a draught-horse enters into the skin of a race-horse, it will be safe to wager that such an anomaly will never win a race, and will fail even to drag a cart. Have we not watched some modern Japanese artists imitating European art? The imitation may sometimes produce clever results; but such cleverness has only the perfection of artificial flowers which never bear fruit.

All great countries have their vital centres for intellectual life, where a high standard of learning is maintained, where the minds of the people are naturally attracted, where they find their genial atmosphere, in which to prove their worth and to contribute their share to the country's culture. Thus they kindle, on the common altar of the land, that great sacrificial fire which can radiate the sacred light of wisdom abroad.

Athens was such a centre in Greece, Rome in Italy; and Paris is such to-day in France.

Benares has been and still continues to be the centre of our Sanskrit culture. But Sanskrit learning does not exhaust all the elements of culture that exist in modern India.

If we were to take for granted, what some people maintain, that Western culture is the only source of light for our mind, then it would be like depending for daybreak upon some star, which is the sun of a far distant sphere. The star may give us light, but not the day; it may give us direction in our voyage of exploration, but it can never open the full view of truth before our eyes. In fact, we can never use this cold starlight for stirring the sap in our branches, and giving colour and bloom to our life. This is the reason why European education has become for India mere school lessons and no culture; a box of matches, good for the small uses of illumination, but not the light of morning, in which the use and beauty, and all the subtle mysteries of life are blended in one.

Let me say clearly that I have no distrust of any culture because of its foreign character. On the contrary, I believe that the shock of such extraneous forces is necessary for the vitality of our intellectual nature. It is admitted that much of the spirit of Christianity runs counter, not only to the classical culture of Europe, but to the European temperament altogether. And yet this alien movement of ideas, constantly running against the natural mental current of Europe, has been a most important factor in strengthening and enriching her civilisation, on account of the sharp antagonism of its intellectual direction. In fact, the European vernaculars first woke up to life and fruitful vigour when they felt the impact of this foreign thought-power with all its oriental forms and affinities. The same thing is happening in India. The European culture has come to us, not only with its knowledge, but with its velocity.

Then, again, let us admit that modern Science is Europe's great gift to humanity for all time to come. We, in India, must claim it from her hands, and gratefully accept it in order to be saved from the curse of futility by lagging behind. We shall fail to reap the harvest of the present age if we delay.

What I object to is the artificial arrangement by which foreign education tends to occupy all the space of our national mind, and thus kills, or hampers, the great opportunity for the creation of a new thought-power by a new combination of truths. It is this which makes me urge that all the elements in our own culture have to be strengthened, not to resist the Western culture, but truly to accept and assimilate it; to use it for our sustenance, not as our burden; to get mastery over this culture, and not to live on its outskirts as the hewers of texts and drawers of book-learning.

The main river in Indian culture has flowed in four streams,—the Vedic, the Puranic, the Buddhist, and the Jain. It has its source in the heights of the Indian consciousness. But a river, belonging to a country, is not fed by its own waters alone. The Tibetan Brahmaputra is a tributary to the Indian Ganges. Contributions have similarly found their way to India's original culture. The Muhammadan, for example, has repeatedly come into India from outside, laden with his own stores of knowledge and feeling and his wonderful religious democracy, bringing freshet after freshet to swell the current. To our music, our architecture, our pictorial art, our literature, the Muhammadans have made their permanent and precious contribution. Those who have studied the lives and writings of our medieval saints, and all the great religious movements that sprang up in the time of the Muhammadan rule, know how deep is our debt to this foreign current that has so intimately mingled with our life.

So, in our centre of Indian learning, we must provide for the co-ordinate study of all these different cultures,—the Vedic, the Puranic, the Buddhist, the Jain, the Islamic, the Sikh and the Zoroastrian. The Chinese, Japanese, and Tibetan will also have to be added; for, in the past, India did not remain isolated within her own boundaries. Therefore, in order to learn what she was, in her relation to the whole continent of Asia, these cultures too must be studied. Side by side with them must finally be placed the Western culture. For only then shall we be able to assimilate this last contribution to our common stock. A river flowing within banks is truly our own, and it can contain its due tributaries; but our relations with a flood can only prove disastrous.

There are some who are exclusively modern, who believe that the past is the bankrupt time, leaving no assets for us, but only a legacy of debts. They refuse to believe that the army which is marching forward can be fed from the rear. It is well to remind such persons that the great ages of renaissance in history were those when man suddenly discovered the seeds of thought in the granary of the past.

The unfortunate people who have lost the harvest of their past have lost their present age. They have missed their seed for cultivation, and go begging for their bare livelihood. We must not imagine that we are one of these disinherited peoples of the world. The time has come for us to break open the treasure-trove of our ancestors, and use it for our commerce of life. Let us, with its help, make our future our own, and not continue our existence as the eternal rag-pickers in other people's dustbins.

So far I have dwelt only upon the intellectual aspect of Education. For, even in the West, it is the intellectual training which receives almost exclusive emphasis. The Western universities have not yet truly recognised that fulness of expression is fulness of life. And a large part of man can never find its expression in the mere language of words. It must therefore seek for its other languages,—lines and colours, sounds and movements. Through our mastery of these we not only make our whole nature articulate, but also understand man in all his attempts to reveal his innermost being in every age and clime. The great use of Education is not merely to collect facts, but to know man and to make oneself known to man. It is the duty of every human being to master, at least to some extent, not only the language of intellect, but also that personality which is the language of Art. It is a great world of reality for man,—vast and profound,—this growing world of his own creative nature. This is the world of Art. To be brought up in ignorance of it is to be deprived of the knowledge and use of that great inheritance of humanity, which has been growing and waiting for every one of us from the beginning of our history. It is to remain deaf to the eternal voice of Man, that speaks to all men the messages that are beyond speech. From the educational point of view we know Europe where it is scientific, or at best literary. So our notion of its modern culture is limited within the boundary lines of grammar and the laboratory. We almost completely ignore the æsthetic life of man, leaving it uncultivated, allowing weeds to grow there. Our newspapers are prolific, our meeting-places are vociferous; and in them we wear to shreds the things we have borrowed from our English teachers. We make the air dismal and damp with the tears of our grievances. But where are our arts, which, like the outbreak of spring flowers, are the spontaneous overflow of our deeper nature and spiritual magnificence?

Through this great deficiency of our modern education, we are condemned to carry to the end a dead load of dumb wisdom. Like miserable outcasts, we are deprived of our place in the festival of culture, and wait at the outer court, where the colours are not for us, nor the forms of delight, nor the songs. Ours is the education of a prison-house, with hard labour and with a drab dress cut to the limits of minimum decency and necessity. We are made to forget that the perfection of colour and form and expression belongs to the perfection of vitality,—that the joy of life is only the other side of the strength of life. The timber merchant may think that the flowers and foliage are mere frivolous decorations of a tree; but if these are suppressed, he will know to his cost that the timber too will fail.

During the Moghal period, music and art in India found a great impetus from the rulers, because their whole life—not merely their official life—was lived in this land; and it is the wholeness of life from which originates Art. But our English teachers are birds of passage; they cackle to us, but do not sing,—their true heart is not in the land of their exile.

Constriction of life, owing to this narrowness of culture, must no longer be encouraged. In the centre of Indian culture which I am proposing, music and art must have their prominent seats of honour, and not be given merely a tolerant nod of recognition. The different systems of music and different schools of art which lie scattered in the different ages and provinces of India, and in the different strata of society, and also those belonging to the other great countries of Asia, which had communication with India, have to be brought there together and studied.

I have already hinted that Education should not be dragged out of its native element, the life-current of the people. Economic life covers the whole width of the fundamental basis of society, because its necessities are the simplest and the most universal. Educational institutions, in order to obtain their fulness of truth, must have close association with this economic life. The highest mission of education is to help us to realise the inner principle of the unity of all knowledge and all the activities of our social and spiritual being. Society in its early stage was held together by its economic co-operation, when all its members felt in unison a natural interest in their right to live. Civilisation could never have been started at all if such was not the case. And civilisation will fall to pieces if it never again realises the spirit of mutual help and the common sharing of benefits in the elemental necessaries of life. The idea of such economic co-operation should be made the basis of our University. It must not only instruct, but live; not only think, but produce.

Our ancient *tapovanas,* or forest schools, which were our natural universities, were not shut off from the daily life of the people. Masters and students gathered fruit and fuel, and took their cattle out to graze, supporting themselves by the work of their own hands. Spiritual education was a part of the spiritual life itself, which comprehended all life. Our centre of culture should not only be the centre of the intellectual life of India, but the centre of her economic life also. It must co-operate with the villages round it, cultivate land, breed cattle, spin cloths, press oil from oil-seeds; it must produce all the necessaries, devising the best means, using the best materials, and calling science to its aid. Its very existence should depend upon the success of its industrial activities carried out on the co-operative principle, which will unite the teachers and students and villagers of the neighbourhood in a living and active bond of necessity. This will give us also a practical industrial training, whose motive force is not the greed of profit.

Before I conclude my paper, a delicate question remains to be considered. What must be the religious ideal that is to rule our centre of Indian culture? The one abiding ideal in the religious life of India has been *Mukti*, the deliverance of man's soul from the grip of self, its communion with the Infinite Soul through its union in *ânanda* with the universe. This religion of spiritual harmony is not a theological doctrine to be taught, as a subject in the class, for half an hour each day. It is the spiritual truth and beauty of our attitude towards our surroundings, our conscious relationship with the Infinite, and the lasting power of the Eternal in the passing moments of our life. Such a religious ideal can only be made possible by making provision for students to live in intimate touch with nature, daily to grow in an atmosphere of service offered to all creatures, tending trees, feeding birds and animals, learning to feel the immense mystery of the soil and water and air.

Along with this, there should be some common sharing of life with the tillers of the soil and the humble workers in the neighbouring villages; studying their crafts, inviting them to the feasts, joining them in works of co-operation for communal welfare; and in our intercourse we should be guided, not by moral maxims or the condescension of social superiority, but by natural sympathy of life for life, and by the sheer necessity of love's sacrifice for its own sake. In such an atmosphere students would learn to understand that humanity is a divine harp of many strings, waiting for its one grand music. Those who realise this unity are made ready for the pilgrimage through the night of suffering, and along the path of sacrifice, to the great meeting of Man in the future, for which the call comes to us across the darkness.

Life, in such a centre, should be simple and clean. We should never believe that simplicity of life might make us unsuited to the requirements of the society of our time. It is the simplicity of the tuning-fork, which is needed all the more because of the intricacy of strings in the instrument. In the morning of our career our nature needs the pure and the perfect note of a spiritual ideal in order to fit us for the complications of our later years.

In other words, this institution should be a perpetual creation by the co-operative enthusiasm of teachers and students, growing with the growth of their soul; a world in itself, self-sustaining, independent, rich with ever-renewing life, radiating life across space and time, attracting and maintaining round it a planetary system of dependent bodies. Its aim should lie in imparting life-breath to the complete man, who is intellectual as well as economic, bound by social bonds, but aspiring towards spiritual freedom and final perfection.

THE END

Printed in Great Britain by R. & R. CLARK, LIMITED, *Edinburgh.*